A PEARL
OF GREAT PRICE

Pearl Kazin Bell

A PEARL
OF GREAT PRICE

The Love Letters
of Dylan Thomas
to Pearl Kazin

Edited and introduced by
Jeff Towns

Afterword by
David Bell

Parthian
The Old Surgery
Napier Street
Cardigan
SA43 1ED
www.parthianbooks.com

First published in 2014
Introduction © Jeff Towns
The Letters of Dylan Thomas © 2014 The Trustees for
the Copyrights of the late Dylan Thomas
The Jester © David Bell

ISBN 978-1-909844-68-1

The publisher acknowledges the financial support of the
Welsh Books Council.

Cover design and typesetting by Claire Houguez

Printed and bound by Gomer Press, Llandysul, Wales

British Library Cataloguing in Publication Data

A cataloguing record for this book is
available from the British Library.

For my friend and mentor Eric Korn and his wife Olga.

The title comes from the *New Testament*: Matthew 13: 45–46

*Again, the kingdom of heaven is like unto a merchant man,
seeking goodly pearls:
Who, when he had found one pearl of great price, went and
sold all that he had, and bought it.*

R. S. Thomas would later use the same phrase in his poem 'The
Bright Field' published in Laboratories of the Spirit (1975)

> *I have seen the sun break through
> to illuminate a small field
> for a while, and gone my way
> and forgotten it. But that was the
> pearl of great price, the one field that had
> treasure in it.*

Contents

The elegant cover of the 1950 Christmas *Harper's* which prints Dylan's *A Child's Christmas in Wales*, commissioned by Pearl Kazin

Introduction: Dylan and Pearl

On a warm, New York spring May day in 1950 a short (he would describe himself as being 'about medium height, above medium height for Wales, I mean...five foot six and a half'), and portly-ish, thirty-five year old Welsh poet and writer, Dylan Thomas, pushed through the plush revolving doors of the opulent head office of *Harper's Bazaar* – the prestigious American fashion monthly, at 572 Madison Avenue, in the heart of bustling downtown Manhattan. He had an appointment with one of the magazine's literary editors probably set up with help from his friend and American agent John Malcolm Brinnin who described himself as Dylan's 'reluctant guardian angel, brother's keeper, nursemaid, amanuensis or bar companion.' It was the poet's first visit to America. He had not been in New York long and he was at the very start of what Brinnin described as 'the rollicking and tragic turmoil of the final four years of his life'.

He was in America to give a series of high-profile readings and lectures to raise some much needed income. He was always short of money, and providing for himself and his wife and three children was a constant struggle. He had never had a regular, paid job, but lived hand to mouth by his pen; selling poems to small magazines; collecting royalties from his books of poems and short stories; picking up commissions for radio scripts and readings on the BBC, hacking out film scripts and relying on the support of a small but loyal and caring group of patrons.

The reason he was visiting *Harper's Bazaar* was to try and sell a piece of work to them for a little extra cash (or for as much as he could squeeze out of this upmarket publication). So he was, if not exactly dressed to kill, definitely looking better than his usual sartorial style, which he himself described as resembling 'an unmade bed'. He shuffled somewhat sheepishly up to the imposing reception desk and asked for Miss Kazin. He was directed to the third floor via the elevator. He proceeded, across the lobby, but only after engaging in some convoluted wordplay with the sassy young secretary over the subtle differences between the English and American languages – 'Oh I just need a lift, I am quite elevated enough,' he boomed in his distinctive Welsh-tinged Queens English.

The plaque outside the door read 'Pearl Kazin: Junior Literary Editor'. Dylan knocked, and was bade to enter by a warm voice that belonged to a highly educated (at Radcliffe, the leading female college of Harvard University), well-dressed and attractive young American. Pearl Kazin was a twenty-seven year old Jewish woman, the sister of the literary critic Alfred Kazin.[*] Pearl had spent a few years teaching English, but was starting to make her own mark on literary New York.

They shook hands across her tidy, but book-laden desk. Pearl offered him coffee with the usual 'How do you take it?', to which

---

[*] Alfred Kazin wrote a very perceptive essay on Dylan Thomas entitled *The Posthumous Life of Dylan Thomas*, first published in *Atlantic Monthly* magazine in 1957 and later included in his collection of critical essays, *Contemporaries*. His essay begins with an intriguing conundrum: 'Dylan Thomas's posthumous life began before he died'.

Dylan winked and smirked cheekily as he replied that what he would most like to take it with was 'a dash of Old Grand-Dad', his new-found favourite bourbon whiskey. After a quick phone call, coffee was brought in and they began exchanging polite but nervous literary small talk, mentioning writers they either both knew or mutually respected. They talked of poets; Theodore Roethke, e e cummings and Marianne Moore, and of the novelist William Faulkner, all of whom Dylan was shortly to meet. But Dylan was there to sell and raise some much needed money, so he carefully steered the conversation towards business. He was taking a chance on offering the magazine a prose piece that had already served him well, but *Harper's* were not to know that. Five years earlier he had written and broadcast *Memories of Christmas* for the BBC. A couple of years later he recast the piece as *Conversation about Christmas* and resold it to *Picture Post*, who published it in their 1947 Christmas edition. He was now trying to sell it yet again. Dylan pulled out a scruffy copy of the manuscript and began to read;

> One Christmas was so much like another, in those years around the seatown corner, out of all sound except the distant speaking of the voices I sometimes hear a moment before sleep...

He paused when he could see that Pearl was transfixed, hypnotised by his words and wallowing in memories of her own childhood holidays. There followed some awkward but polite and gentle negotiating on both sides, before Pearl put a call upstairs to her boss, Mary Louis Aswell,[*] who trusted and supported her

---

[*] The literary editor at *Harper's* was the legendary Mary Louise Aswell, a Philadelphia Quaker who treated Pearl as something of an adoptive daughter and the same 'Mary Lou' was later to be godmother to Pearl's son David.

protégé's judgement, and Pearl eventually bought the story from a happy and relieved Welsh poet for $300.*

Dylan then began mumbling and with some embarrassment, asked if there was any chance of the fee in cash, and if payment could be made on the spot. Pearl obliged and after a quick call to accounts the bills arrived as swift as the coffee.

Pearl was already taken by the boyish, innocent charm of this somewhat older, but charming elfin poet from Wales. He for his part was smitten by her too, so business done, he began to flirt, but not in his usual somewhat course and direct manner, he already felt that Pearl would not be impressed with that approach.

Pearl asked Dylan if he still spoke his native tongue and, instead of his usual off-hand dismissal of the first language of both his parents, he spoke of his loss of Welsh as a great disappointment, to which she admitted that her first language

---

* It was eventually published in *Harper's Bazaar* in December 1950. Ferris in a footnote in *The Letters* mentions a memo from Ann Watkins, who was Dylan's New York literary agent, to his London agent David Higham on May 24th 1950, which informed them that '[Thomas] has personally sold a prose story to Pearl Kazin of *Harper's Bazaar...*' Both Thomas' bibliographers – J. Alexander Rolph and Ralph Maud give the title of this printing as *A Child's Memories of Christmas in Wales*, which would suggest they had never seen the original magazine where a look at the contents page and the printed story would indicate that Dylan, and/or Pearl had named it for the first time as *A Child's Christmas in Wales*. Ferris acknowledges that 'This quick carpentry work created one of his most popular works' and stresses again that as '*A Child's Christmas in Wales*, this probably has come to appeal to a wider audience, both in print and as a recording than anything else he wrote'. It is worth noting that when Dylan was recording this piece for his first LP for Caedmon in New York later that year, it was the *Harper's Bazaar* magazine that he read from; Pearl's role as the literary godmother of *A Child's Christmas...* cannot be overstated.

was Yiddish, but that in her case she was proud to still be fluent in an elegant, literary Yiddish. Their conversation moved towards politics and Dylan probed as to where she aligned herself and he was surprised and pleased when she admitted that she had belonged to the Young Communist League while in high school so he told her about his old Swansea pal and political mentor Bert Trick, 'the communist grocer'. He explained his own youthful flirtations with the far left but admitted that he was never a communist with a capital C. She was impressed. However when he regaled her with a rather exaggerated account of his involvement in an anti-fascist rally against Oswald Moseley and his Black-Shirts back in pre-war Swansea, Dylan, who never shied from hyperbole laid it on thick and presented himself as a brave and fearless partisan. The air of intimacy between them was enhanced by Pearl's hushed, conspiratorial, almost whispering tone of speech, for this was the beginning of the era of McCarthyism* in America and the hallowed offices of *Harper's Bazaar* were no place for discussions involving Jewish nationalism, Yiddish and communism.

Pearl then began to admit with some embarrassment of her own that while at college she had taken elocution lessons to eradicate her Brooklyn twang only for Dylan to confess that he too had been sent to elocution as a child to soften his Swansea Welsh accent. And it transpired that they had yet more in common; they had both left education for journalism. Dylan amused her by regaling

---

* The first recorded use of the term McCarthyism was in a political cartoon in the Washington Post. Their cartoonist Herbert Block, who signed himself Herblock, published on March 29th, 1950, a cartoon which depicted four leading Republicans trying to push an elephant (the traditional symbol of the Republican Party) up onto a teetering stack of ten tar buckets, the topmost of which was labelled 'McCarthyism'.

her with tales of his time as 'Ace newshound two typewriter Thomas' during his notorious days on the *South Wales Evening Post*, stories that he had drawn upon for some of his finest short stories in *Portrait of the Artist as a Young Dog*.

When Pearl explained to him that one of the reasons she had left academia for journalism was in order to be able to move back to her native New York, which she missed so much, it prompted Dylan to explain his own deep love of Swansea and Wales and to elaborate at length on the romantic Welsh notion of 'Hiraeth'. Pearl was both fascinated and entranced.

There conversation moved seamlessly and endlessly but Dylan realised he had perhaps stayed too long and got up to leave, offering his pudgy hand across her desk, he thanked Pearl for her time and efforts on his behalf and then he nervously suggested that they might meet up for a drink at the San Remo – a new bar Dylan had discovered in Greenwich Village that was both a change from, and also a bit more salubrious than his regular haunt, The White Horse Tavern. To his surprise she accepted. Thanking her again and bowing graciously he backed out of her office and surprised himself by unconsciously foregoing the elevator and descending via the echoing stairwell whistling 'Men of Harlech' as he went. He spun through the revolving doors and out into the bright Spring sunshine and ambled along Madison Avenue with a new spring in his step, very pleased with his morning's success on many levels.

Some of the above is true, but only the bare facts; Pearl was a literary editor at *Harper's Bazaar*, and Dylan Thomas did visit her; she did take his Christmas story, and it was published in the December 1950 issue of *Harper's Bazaar*. The rest is a fiction I have constructed because neither party wrote an account of this first meeting and there were no other witnesses. But an intense and passionate relationship did begin on that day and we know this because one side of their correspondence has survived. Six 'love letters' sent from Dylan to Pearl. These, together with a couple of snapshots of them looking happy together in London and a book of poetry by Yeats bearing a warm inscription from Dylan to Pearl, provide us with evidence enough. We know she sent him letters; Dylan makes many references to them in his letters, but they have not survived.

Until these letters came to light Pearl had remained something of a ghost. Indeed Pearl was at first hidden behind the name 'Sarah', and even though this would become Pearl in later biographies, her full name was not used in any Dylan Thomas books until 2000 when Paul Ferris uses it in his new edition of the *Collected Letters*. In his introduction he also notes that,

> [Dylan's] correspondence with mistresses is thin – although a group of letters to an American lover has come on the market in a furtive sort of way, with a condition attached that they must not be published.

This is a reference to the letters published here.

We can however glean something of Pearl's side of the story from John Malcolm Brinnin's *Dylan Thomas in America*, a book which caused quite a stir when it was published in 1955 in America (1956 in Britain), just a few years after Dylan's death in New York in 1953. It became quite a *cause célèbre*, especially in the UK. It was one of the first of a new style of biographical writing; no-holds-barred, kiss-an'-tell, full disclosure, which nowadays is the norm. But in the fifties the book caused a sensation. Vernon Watkins was so distressed by the book that he refused to allow J. M. Dent, the British publishers of the book, to publish his correspondence with Dylan (eventually a compromise was reached which saw that book would have two publishers' names on the title page with Vernon's Faber & Faber first). Caitlin Thomas wrote a disclaimer that all copies of the book carried,[*] Edith Sitwell wrote a fierce review of the book in the *Sunday Times* and the columns of the *Times Literary Supplement* carried a feisty correspondence for a few weeks in the aftermath.

Brinnin, in an act of loyalty to his friend, refers to Pearl as 'Sarah' and includes her among two other unidentified New York 'lady-friends' of Dylan's, however she does not make it into the index (which only appears in the US edition). From the first mention 'Sarah' is marked out as special. Brinnin writes that her main rival 'Doris', 'was frankly a passing fancy', and he goes on to state

> but with Sarah he fell in love, with consequences that were to disturb him profoundly for more than a year.

Pearl was something of a friend of Brinnin in that they inhabited the same New York literary and social milieu, but he was not in any way acting as a 'gondolier' in their meeting. He writes of her, in comparison with other of Dylan's women-friends,

> Sarah was vastly different in manner, substance and background. She held an important job in publishing to which she brought an extraordinary sense of intelligence, an executive sense of responsibility, and that air of professional sophistication governed by the Madison Avenue fashion journals. She had been highly educated, had taught for several years at one of the leading woman's colleges, and was knowledgeably devoted to Dylan's work from the time of its earliest publication.

---

[*]   In a new preface to a 1989 reprint of the book, Brinnin writes that, during a later encounter with Dylan's friend Ruthven Todd in Palma, Spain, he regretted having just missed meeting Caitlin, who had just left. Brinnin writes that he learned from Ruthven that 'Caitlin found my copy of *Dylan Thomas in America*... One morning, book in hand, she came to breakfast. Know what she said? "Dear funny old John, his fucking book isn't nearly as bad as I had thought." Can you believe, all these years, she's never read it.'

He sums up this testimonial with a somewhat oblique but telling observation,

> These qualities, combined with her dark handsomeness and social poise, made her precisely the sort of woman from whom one would expect Dylan only to flee.

And he ends by admitting,

> How deep he felt about her I did not then know, since neither he nor Sarah confided in me except to let me know that they were lovers.

Brinnin's book offers no further details about Dylan and Pearl, until he is describing Dylan's departure aboard the liner the *Queen Elizabeth*, at the end of his momentous first reading tour, and the hectic and lively farewell party that lasted right up until the gangplank was raised and Dylan's non-travelling friends had to scamper ashore. Brinnin's account ends with a sad and moving description of Pearl,

> When the abysmal whistle blew and the gangplank was hauled up, I stood alone in a dim corner of Pier 90, feeling not only parting sadness but a suddenly overwhelming wave of desolation. As the ship began to move away, I noticed Sarah standing quite by herself far away from me, quietly weeping. When she ran toward me, we embraced in an absurd and wordless flood of tears as the *Queen Elizabeth* backed into the wash of her propellers and began to slide out to sea.

Pearl occurs again in Brinnin's book when he is writing of his visit to London in August 1950,

> I went to Europe in late August... Dylan would be waiting for me when the boat-train pulled into Paddington station. My first sight of him showed me a new man: his clothes were new and well-matched, his shoes glinted with a high shine, [and] his face was serene and ruddy.

He later realises that this new scrubbed-up Dylan is especially for Pearl, who is on her way to London,

> Sarah was now at sea on her way to England having cabled Dylan to say that she would arrive in London on September 4th.

However, once she arrives, Brinnin is discretion personified. After the couple fail to show up for dinner with Brinnin and the critic Harry T. Moore at Wheeler's in Soho, Brinnin dines with the critic alone but when he returns to his hotel he finds,

> ...a telephone note from Dylan asking me to join him and Sarah at the Café Royal. I hurried to Piccadilly and found them in a gilt and plush bar. Dylan seemed happy to see Sarah again, treated her with the same welcoming committee eagerness to please with which he had greeted me, but he was obviously most interested in being alone with her. I left after one drink.

He is with them again the next day during which the only surviving pictures of Dylan and Pearl were taken. According to Brinnin,

> Next afternoon we met, all three at the Salisbury* drank gin and lime and strolled through crowded streets toward the Embankment. There, on Dylan's suggestion, we took a river bus down the Thames to a point beyond Greenwich. It was a grey day on the busy river and Sarah and I enjoyed being tourists and asking Dylan to identify all the domes and towers we saw. There was a little bar on the riverboat; we took our drinks out on deck as we chugged among outgoing tramp steamers, coal-laden barges and puffing

---

* A vast pub, an opulent temple of Victoriana, all cut glass mahogany and chandeliers on St Martins Lane. It is where Bill Brandt took one of his most famous photographs of Dylan Thomas.

tugboats. We took snapshots... It was a fine festive little excursion, but in spite of outbursts of his high explosive laughter, Dylan was for most of the time gloomy and troubled. At one point, when Sarah had gone to fetch us drinks from the bar, he turned to me:

'John, what am I going to do?'

His face suddenly sober, showed bewilderment and his eyes were set on something far away.

'About what?'

'I'm in love with Sarah, and I am in love with my wife. I don't know what to do.'

Brinnin's response is both honest and perceptive;

It was a question no one could have answered save himself and I did not attempt to. But this was a new confidence, and my first experience of seeing Dylan wrestling with a problem rather than seeking out a means to circumvent it.

Brinnin; at this point, concludes;

Like the illicit lovers of a thousand English novels, they were going off to Brighton for a day or two; I was flying to Paris in the morning...

In a subsequent chapter Brinnin tells his version of the 'end of the affair'. He hears nothing directly from Dylan for seven months but gets 'the only news of him from "Sarah".' He learns from her that after Brighton she had gone to France, but suddenly Dylan was not responding to her letters and messages 'sent to Dylan at the Savage club where he usually received all his London mail.' She returned to London in October where she had expected to meet up with Dylan again but this was not to be. Brinnin sums the situation up,

She stayed in London for some weeks, learned that Dylan was ill and could not be seen and, finally, in the continued absence of any word from him at all, left for

Greece feeling betrayed and unwanted. When she wrote to me expressing incomprehension at Dylan's neglect of her, I wrote to say that I was convinced there had been some large misunderstanding. I was sure that Dylan could not intentionally be unkind, especially toward her, and I asked her to stave off disillusion until the facts could be known. To remind her of the day on which Dylan declared to me his her love for her, I enclosed some of the snapshots.

He then quotes at length from a letter Pearl sent him the following January in which she gives him her account of what had happened;

Your letter gave me as much delight as anything that's happened to me recently... And the pictures, which in my happy timeless suspension, here seem to have been taken centuries ago, are wonderful to have, and help eradicate the woes of my second London [trip] quite entirely... I wrote you a whining little note last week... that crossed your fine envelope packed with the best, and I spoke in that of a letter from Dylan. And the explanation did lie, as he discovered only when he got my letters from here, and as I suspected all the time, in the fine Italian hand of the grey lady, —. I won't attempt to tell it all here, and there's no need, but Dylan was ill...all the time I was in London and she collected his mail for him at the Savage every morning. What she did with them neither of us will probably know, but he saw none of my messages or letters, nothing. She came to see me off at the air station when I finally did give up and go back to France, laden with her flowers and dulcet doom, even now she sends me poisonously cheerful letters about how lucky I am to be out of England. But that's the end of it now, with all its soap-opera bubbles broken, finally.

Dylan and Pearl. London, September 1950.

Pearl Kazin and Dylan Thomas share a newspaper on the Thames Embankment – looking for a Marx Brothers film to watch that evening?

Pearl
Dylan
London
September
1950
love

Dylan's gift to Sarah. A copy of Yeats's Poems inscribed, by Dylan to her, with 'love'.

Brinnin adds his own comments,

> This last sentence was Sarah's epitaph for a romance which, as time would tell, had irrevocably foundered, partly through plotted intervention, partly through Dylan's inability to deal maturely with his feelings or to recognise their consequences.

Brinnin then quotes from a later letter from Dylan in which he seems well over the affair, although there is an element of false bravado in his hyperbolic self loathing,

> I remember the Thames and old Sarah – whom I saw something of later but who, I imagine, left London, as I imagined you had done, rasping to herself:
>
> 'No more of that beer cheapened hoddy-noddy, snoring, paunched, his corn, sick, his fibs, I'm off to Greece where you know where you are; oh, his sodden bounce, his mis-theatrical-demeanor, the boastful tuppence.'
>
> I haven't heard from her since she went away...

However, despite this, towards the end of the letter, he asks Brinnin to pass on 'his love' to a list of New York friends, and the first on the list is 'Pearl'.

And now these six letters, first published here, give a glimpse of Dylan's side of the story. Those interested can find more details and background in the subsequent biographies; the 'official' 1965 biography by Constantine Fitzgibbon was followed just over a decade later by the work of the pre-eminent Dylan Thomas aficionado Paul Ferris, who grew up and was schooled in the same Swansea places as Dylan. He produced his first intensively researched biography in 1977 and revised and enlarged it in 1999. He also wrote a biography of Caitlin at her behest in 1993, and edited the monumental *Dylan Thomas: The Collected Letters* in 1985, which he also revised and enlarged in 2000. Finally Andrew Lycett found sufficient new and pertinent materials to produce another hefty volume *Dylan Thomas – A New Life* in 2003 to mark the fiftieth anniversary of the poet's death in New York.

Other related literary memoirs and letters – particularly those of the American poets Elizabeth Bishop[*] and John Berryman[**] – also fill in gaps in the story, but many of these are sad, tragic even, and some are quite sordid and unseemly, especially those found in Caitlin's brutally honest, but sometimes just plain brutal, autobiography, *Caitlin: Life with Dylan Thomas – A Warring Absence*, which was compiled and edited by George Tremlett from many hours of tape recorded interviews he made with her in 1985. (The book was published a year later.)

These letters add something to the dates, details and facts contained in these books, but they also indicate that the relationship was more serious, that it lasted longer, and that it had a profound effect on Dylan's life, and in turn, was an inadvertent contributory factor in his sad and untimely death.

Pearl's letter to Brinnin was sent in the January of 1951 and it would seem to indicate the end of the affair – 'But that's the end of it now, with all its soap-opera bubbles broken, finally.' She also writes of the unidentified 'grey lady'. We know that this is Margaret Taylor, the eccentric and flighty wife of the historian A.J.P. Taylor. As a rich patron she provided almost all of the many houses that Dylan and his family lived in. But she was also infatuated with Dylan and we know that not only did she intercept Dylan's mail but, spurred on as much by her own jealously of Pearl, she rushed to Laugharne and shared in a cruel and malicious way all she knew of Dylan and Pearl with Caitlin.

The result was all and worse than one would expect; never have the words of William Congreve, spoken by Zara in his seventeenth

---

[*]   *One Art: Elizabeth Bishop*. Letters selected and edited by Robert Giroux in 1994.
[**] *Dream Song: The Life of John Berryman*, Paul Mariani, 1990.

century play *The Mourning Bride*, been more fully realised,

> Heav'n has no Rage, like Love to Hatred turn'd,
> Nor Hell a Fury, like a Woman scorn'd'.

Dylan knew nothing of Margaret's actions. He arrived home to be confronted by Caitlin's furious rage aand violent physical assaults. He was deeply shocked, afraid, and ill-prepared. His damage limitation was a knee-jerk reaction of panic and denial, which shows in this imploring letter to Helen McAlpine – Caitlin's closest friend – begging and pleading for her support.

Sent on Sept 14th 1950,

Helen

I came back to find Caitlin terribly distressed but managed to tell her that all that the grey fiend had pumped into her ear was lies and poison. And so it was. And Cat believed me. And now we are happy, as always, together again and that other thing is over for ever. So, please Helen: remember for Cat's sake if not mine; All, all, that grey scum said was LIES. When Cat asks you, as she will, you must, please say: 'It is all LIES. I met a girl with Dylan & that is all there was to it.' You must, Helen please. Don't answer this... Do destroy this. I trust you & my dear Bill implicitly, as you know. All was LIES. And incidentally it was. And incidentally, the girl has gone to France, not to return.

Ever Dylan

Here Pearl's kindly 'grey lady', who sends her 'flowers and dulcet doom' and 'poisonously cheerful letters', is branded by Dylan as the 'grey fiend' and 'grey scum'. Ferris' footnote to the letter is short and succinct:

The Thomases were having a marital crisis. The 'grey fiend' was Margaret Taylor, who had hurried to Laugharne with the news that Dylan was involved with a New York magazine executive Pearl Kazin.

Despite all this trauma Dylan sends Pearl a further two letters after this, the first a heart-rending attempt to explain himself which ends with a tortured afterthought,

> Oh, what a snivelling note to you, my darling, when I could write two Wars & Peaces. Believe in me. I'm nasty, but I adore you. I wouldn't hurt you. Nothing is impossible for us: it can't be. And out of everything we'll make, somehow, some happiness together again & again & again till the end of whatever. But, still, I cannot forgive myself for not having written so long before this. It is not for want of thinking of you, my Pearl. Every moment I do, of every hour.

And they do see each other however briefly on Dylan's subsequent tours to America. Pearl attended Dylan's final reading in his second lecture tour (where he was accompanied by Caitlin) and met him afterwards, and they see each other again in Boston on his third tour in 1952, and she was also in the audience for the first stage performance of *Under Milk Wood* * on 14th May 1952. They spent a little time together over the next few days, but by then Dylan's relationship with Liz Reitell, his current PA and 'producer' of *Under Milk Wood*, was becoming closer.

Pearl and Dylan shared a friendship with the poet Elizabeth Bishop who From 1949 to 1950, was the Consultant in Poetry for the Library of Congress, and in that capacity she had met and made recordings of Dylan reading. Pearl and Elizabeth were very close and she was also part of Dylan's New York circle – Loren MacIver the painter and Lloyd Frankenberg her partner, Brinnin and also Robert Lowell. In a letter from Paris that Bishop sent to Loren MacIver in October 1950 she can't resist sharing the gossip that she has heard

---

* There is one further connection between Pearl and Dylan but it is in print rather than in person – see Appendix.

from Joe Frank 'that Pearl and Dylan are the talk of the town, etc'.

But it is her letter to Pearl just after Dylan's death that is worth quoting at length, it was sent from Brazil on November 16th 1953,

> Lota just came back...when we sat down to lunch she opened *Times*...and there was the notice about [the death of] Dylan Thomas. Just a few lines, saying 'of undisclosed causes...in Manhattan'. It must have happened just before they went to press, or surely there would have been more in the 'news' section. Good lord – I suppose it must be true, but I can't believe it yet. My imagination keeps rushing from horror to horror because of the way that awful *Times* put it. Oh Pearl, it is so tragic. I hope you are not too upset by it, by whatever did happen to him – if anyone knows – and I hope you will be able to write and tell me what did. I want to know and I don't know anyone else I can ask. The first time I met Dylan, when he spent the day with me doing those recordings in Washington, he and Joe Frank and I had lunch together, and even after knowing him for three or four hours I felt frightened for him and depressed. But I found him so tremendously sympathetic at the same time. I said to Joe later something trite about 'Why he'll kill himself if he goes on like this,' and Joe said promptly, 'Don't be silly. Can't you see a man like that does not want to live? I give him another two or three years.' And I suppose everyone felt that way, but I don't know enough about him really to understand why. Why do some poets manage to get by and live to be malicious old bores like Frost or – probably – pompous old ones like Yeats, or crazy old ones like Pound – and some just don't! But his poetry has that desperate win-or-lose-all quality, of course – and of course it too eliminates everything from life except something beyond human supportability after a while. But why oh why did he

have to go & die now? Was he unhappy with those readings? I wonder. Or recent work? I think there's a new book with some poems in it I haven't seen yet. Poets should have self-doubts left out of their systems completely – as one can see most of the serving ones seem to have. But look at poor Cal – and Marianne, who hangs on just by the skin of her teeth and the most appalling paranoia I've ever heard of. And of course it isn't just poets. We're all wretched and half the time or three quarters I think it is a thoroughly disgusting world – and then the horror vanishes for a while, mercifully. But in my own minor way I know enough about drink & destruction. Please, Pearl, tell me what happened to the poor man, if you know – and can bear to... I have been thinking about you a lot – even dreaming, you see, – and I was worried about how you were ... And now this sad awful news. I have no way of knowing how you felt about it recently or what your feelings about Dylan were. I think I had expected to hear news like that at any time, but even so it is a bad shock... But please write and tell me everything if you can. I have met few people in my life I felt such an instantaneous sympathy for, and although there must have been many things wrong, Dylan made most of our contemporaries seem small and disgustingly self-seeking and cautious and cold.

On Dylan's final fatal trip to New York, after his collapse at the Chelsea Hotel he was admitted to St Vincents Hospital on November 5th. He was in a coma from which he did not recover. News of his condition was carried in the press throughout the world and Pearl would have been well aware of it. In the days before Dylan's death Pearl was at a literary conference at Bard College in Annandale-on-Hudson. On the night of the 7th, she was at a campus party with

Ralph Ellison,[*] Saul Bellow[**] and the poet John Berryman.[***]

Berryman was one of Dylan's friends and a passionate admirer of his writings. Berryman was already deeply troubled by Dylan's plight and was ranting aloud about the imminent loss 'one of the greatest lyric poets who had ever lived'. Paul Mariani takes up the sad story in his biography of Berryman, *Dream Song*,

> The following night, as the conference ended with yet another party, Berryman and Kazin kept telephoning St. Vincent's, trying to get information on Thomas's condition. Ellison heard Berryman 'relieve himself of a rather drunken recital of "Do Not Go Gentle Into That Good Night"' and later that evening drove Berryman and Kazin back to New York. It was midnight when they reached the hotel, but Berryman insisted that he and Pearl go directly to St Vincent's. Ellison dropped them off but did not go in with them, 'because their grief was so intensely private'. Though it was late, the sister on duty let the two in to see Dylan, who lay in the darkened room under an oxygen tent lying eerily still.

The next day, November 9th 1953, Dylan died and Pearl was left with her memories – and the letters published here.

---

[*] Pearl Kazin was one of the first to publish sections of Ralph Ellison's important novel *Invisible Man*, which addressed many of the social and intellectual issues facing African-Americans early in the twentieth century.

[**] Saul Bellow was the Canadian-born novelist who won the Nobel Prize for Literature in 1976.

[***] John Berryman returned to the hospital the next day alone and went again into Dylan's room, where he found Dylan unattended. As he looked at him he realised with great horror and shock that something was wrong. In panic he shouted for a nurse, who appeared, and on examining Dylan, pronounced him dead. Berryman never really recovered from this and twenty years later, aged fifty-eight, he jumped to his death from a bridge over the Mississippi River.

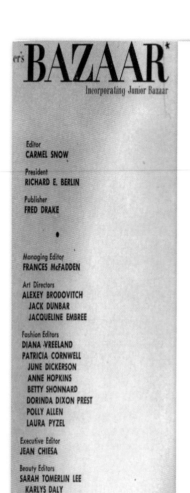

er's **BAZAAR***

Incorporating Junior Bazaar

Editor
CARMEL SNOW

President
RICHARD E. BERLIN

Publisher
FRED DRAKE

•

Managing Editor
FRANCES McFADDEN

Art Directors
ALEXEY BRODOVITCH
JACK DUNBAR
JACQUELINE EMBREE

Fashion Editors
DIANA VREELAND
PATRICIA CORNWELL
JUNE DICKERSON
ANNE HOPKINS
BETTY SHONNARD
DORINDA DIXON PREST
POLLY ALLEN
LAURA PYZEL

Executive Editor
JEAN CHIESA

Beauty Editors
SARAH TOMERLIN LEE
KARLYS DALY

Fiction Editors
MARY LOUISE ASWELL
PEARL KAZIN

The contents page of the December issue. Pearl is listed on the bottom left as a Fiction Editor. Dylan's story is first up. Did Pearl write the brief Christmas Editorial where Dylan's piece is described as 'a child's Christmas, tenderly remembered'?

A CHILD'S
CHRISTMAS
IN WALES

by Dylan Thomas

One Christmas was so much like another, in those years around the seatown corner, out of all sound except the distant speaking of the voices I sometimes hear a moment before sleep; that I can never remember whether it snowed for six days and six nights when I was twelve or whether it snowed for twelve days and twelve nights when I was six. All the Christmases roll down toward the two-tongued sea, like a cold and headlong moon bundling down the sky that was our street; and they stop at the rim of the ice-edged, fish-freezing waves, and I plunge my hands in the snow and bring out whatever I can find. In goes my hand into that wool-white bell-tongued ball of holidays resting at the rim of the carol-singing sea, and out come Mrs. Prothero and the firemen.

It was on the afternoon of the day of Christmas Eve, and I was in Mrs. Prothero's garden, waiting for cats, with her son Jim. It was snowing. It was always snowing at Christmas. December, in my memory, is white as Lapland, though there were no reindeers. But there were cats. Patient, cold and callous, our hands wrapped in socks, we waited to snowball the cats. Sleek and long as jaguars and horrible-whiskered, spitting and snarling, they would slink and sidle over the white back-garden walls, and the lynx-eyed hunters, Jim and I, fur-capped and moccasined trappers from Hudson Bay, off Mumbles Road, would hurl our deadly snowballs at the green of their eyes. The wise cats never appeared. We were so still, Eskimo-footed arctic marksmen in the muffling silence of the eternal snows—eternal, ever since Wednesday—that we never heard Mrs. Prothero's first cry from her igloo at the bottom of the garden. Or, if we heard it at all, it was, to us, like the far-off challenge of our enemy and prey, the neighbor's Polar cat. But soon the voice grew louder. "Fire!" cried Mrs. Prothero, and she beat the dinner-gong. And we ran down the garden, with the snowballs in our arms, toward the house; and smoke, indeed, was pouring out of the dining room, and the gong was bombilating, and Mrs. Prothero was announcing ruin like a town crier in Pompeii. This was better than all the cats in Wales standing on the wall in a row. We bounded into the house, laden with snowballs, and stopped at the open door of the smoke-filled room. Something was burning all right; perhaps it was Mr. Prothero, who always slept there after midday dinner with a newspaper over his face. But he was standing in the middle of the room, saying, "A fine Christmas!" and smacking at the smoke with a slipper. "Call the fire brigade," cried Mrs. Prothero as she beat the gong. "They won't be here," said Mr. Prothero, "it's Christmas." There was no fire to be seen, only clouds of smoke and Mr. Prothero standing in the middle of them,

The Letters

Pearl's apologies to Frances Hammel: 'I dropped
it onto a wet floor twenty-one years ago...'

Letter One

June 22nd 1950. Sent from the Savage Club

Miss Pearl Kazin,
Harper's Bazaar,
572 Madison Avenue,
New York 22,
N.Y.
U.S.A.

June 28, 1950

Pearl darling, my
love you most truly. I miss
There were forty eight st...
when I arrived but when I
added. the state 5 ...
you forgotten me? I'm
building ...rcher who
on your way to work,
talk too warm as ...
sharp as sciatic...
blowlamp ... la...
went with you to th...
remember? Wild as
to take you to rag...
bloody hills. I w...
I kissed you in th...
will you write th...
or don't you want to write or have you said,
To hell. I wanted only you to see me off on
that shiny, floating doldrum, and there
was Mrs Williams, producing ectoplasm to order
like a waiter dishing up spaghetti, and the
psychoanalyst's wife, his unfinished homework
and so many others. The ship was hell. My
rathole cabin sharer was called, so far as
I could gather, Urine. I sat, at meals, with
two pig business men on their way to Paree,
with nudges, a well-kept harpy who had, but
fortunately at other tables, seventeen giggling
girls in her charge and who was to show
them Europe in three weeks, Urine himself,
who represents cement, and a dried hen
who'd been clucking for Unesco. I sat in the
bar all day, listening to stories about
Scotchmen, Irishmen, & Jews, bridal nights,
contraceptives, adultery, drunkenness, and the
movements of the bowels. Your friend... I

The Savage Club
1 Carlton House Terrace
London

June 22 1950,

Pearl Darling , my [...] love you most truly. I miss you [...]
There were forty eight st [...] when I arrived but when I [...]
added. the state I was [...] you forgotten me [...]

I'm [...] who [...] on your way to work, [...] talk too, warm
as [...] sharp as [...] blowlamp [...] went with you to the [...]
remember? Wild as [...] to take you to [...] bloody [...] I [...]
I [...] kissed you in the [...] will you write to me [...] Or don't
you want to write or have you said, To hell. I wanted only
you to see me off on that shiny, floating doldrum, and there
was Mrs Williams producing ectoplasm to order like a
waiter dishing up spaghetti; and the psychoanalyst's wife,
his unfinished homework, and so many others. The ship was
hell. My rathole cabin-sharer was called so far as I could
gather, Urine. I sat, at meals, with two pig business men on
their way to Paree, with nudges, a well-kept harpy who had,
but fortunately at other tables, seventeen giggling girls in her
charge and who was to show them Europe in three weeks,
Urine himself, who represents cement, and a dried hen who'd
been clucking for Unesco. I sat in the bar all day, listening
to stories about Scotchmen, Irishmen, & Jews, bridal nights,
contraceptives, adultery, drunkenness and the movements of
the bowels. Your friend, who I

liked, with the two children, I saw hardly at all.
I did not see the sea for days. I thought about you
very, very much, and wanted to be with you, as I
want to be with you now. Nobody met me at London,
which was not surprising as nobody knew I
would be there, or cared ~~whether~~, and the town
was hot and sticky and nobody, in my
favourite pubs, asked me where I'd been. Oh,
the lonliness, for you, and the pity, for me,
oozing through the lost streets. I very nearly
flew back, at once, to howl through Brooklyn for
~~with~~ you. After a week in London, I came
down here, to the country, but am going back
to London tomorrow, to my reactionary, red-
nosed club. Please write me there, if you want to
write.
And could it be true that you might, in September,
come to England first? You said it might. And
I would meet you, gardenia in buttonhole, with
a gold hat, dancing and roaring, at Southampton
or London. Whenever you come, I shall meet
you. But let it be soon.
What shall I tell you? You know all about it.
                    I'm writing a poem I shall send
you, though not for the rich Bazaar.
                    And I'll sit in the Savage,
drinking Punch and reading sherry, until your
letter comes. The world is empty this side of the
damned sea.
Last night, I opened the door of a car on the
wrong side, and fell in a pond. Nothing else has
happened to me.
I am writing in a draughty box above some
herons.
I love you

                                Dylan.

liked, with the two children I hardly saw at all. I did not see the sea for days. I thought about you very, very much, and wanted to be with you, as I want to be with you now. Nobody met me at London, which was not surprising as nobody knew I would be there, or cared, and the town was hot and sticky and nobody, in my favourite pubs, asked me where I'd been. Oh, the loneliness, for you, and the pity, for me, oozing through the lost streets. I very nearly flew back, at once, to howl through Brooklyn for you. After a week in London, I came down here, to the country, but I am going back to London tomorrow, to my reactionary red-nosed club. Please write to me there, if you want to write.

And could it be true that you might, in September, come to England first? You said it might. And I would meet you, gardenia in buttonhole, with a gold hat, dancing and leering, at Southampton or London. Whenever you come, I shall meet you. But let it be soon.

What shall I tell you? You know all about it.

I'm writing a poem I shall send you, though not for the rich Bazaar.

And I'll sit in the Savage, drinking Punch and reading sherry, until your letter comes. The world is empty this side of the damned sea.

Last night, I opened the door of a car on the wrong side, and fell in a pond. Nothing else has happened to me.

I am writing in a draughty box above some herons.

I love you.

Dylan.

Letter Two

August 7th, 1950. The Savage Club, London.

August 7, 1950

Pearl.
It's taken so long to write your name. Pearl,
dear Pearl.
And every moment of every day I think of you, I
feel you, I want you, I talk to you silent and
alone. My very dear Pearl, my love.
                all the seconds before and since your
lonely last letter (oh, thank you, Pearl darling),
I've tried to write to you, I've tried to say
who and what you are to me, but didn't know
the words. You are the reason for everything
that is, except Korea, Formosa, McArthur, all
governments and all wicked people. Many
times, many times, in this boiled club, in the
sad country, on trains, in the pits of
dejection, or happy as nothing just to know
that you are alive, I've tried to write, but
was suddenly shy. Even when I read, again
and again, your most loving letters, through
which you looked at me, I was still shy
as a badger when it came to putting
down, to sealing in an envelope, to sending
over the fishy sea, " I love you". But now
I have said it, I can again and again (I
love you, Pearl) and I wonder how under the
sun I couldn't have said, a hundred times
over, such a simple enormous, and deeper
than the Atlantic truth.
I feel, some times, so close to you that the
earth stops, the seas dry up, and across the
deep dust I can kiss you.

August 7, 1950

The Savage Club
1 Carlton House
Terrace,
London, S. W. 3.

Pearl.

It's taken so long to write your name. Pearl, dear Pearl.

And every moment of every day I think of you. I feel you, I want you, I talk to you silent and alone. My very dear Pearl, my love.

All the seconds before and since your lonely last letter (oh, thank you, Pearl darling), I've tried to write to you, I've tried to say who and what you are to me, but didn't know the words. You are the reason for everything that is, except Korea, Formosa, McArthur, all governments and all the wicked people. Many times, many times, in this boiled club, in the sad country, on trains, in the pits of dejection, or happy as nothing just to know that you are alive, I've tried to write, but was suddenly shy. Even when I read, again and again, your most loving letters, through which you looked at me, I was still shy as a badger when it came to putting down, to sealing in an envelope, to sending over the fishy sea "I love you". But now I have said it, I can again and again (I love you, Pearl) and I wonder how under the sun I couldn't have said, a hundred times over, such a simple, enormous, and deeper than the atlantic truth.

I feel, some times, so close to you that the earth stops, the seas dry up, and across the deep dust I can kiss you.

And all the things, too, in my life, now, involve
you from head to foot. I wish your head were
in my arms, as I sit mooning here, but
I should be glad if your body, which I
adore, were joined on to it. Smile secretly
for me, as I, salted with loneliness, am
smiling for you as I write: to the surprise
of a pickled member: I mean, a man who
looks pickled, and who's reading Punch
upside down in a doldrum. Smile for me,
Pearl my true dear, wherever you read this.
When your last letter came, I snuggled it
around, under my coat, for hours, gloating,
before I dare open it: no, not only gloating,
for I was terrified too: perhaps you were
dead (though I ~~would have known~~), or
forgetful, or censorious, for I am always,
my love, a little scared of you, which is
only as it should be, I never really
daring to dream that you could be fond of
me as I am fond — good god, "fond"
for what shakes my body and my world —
of you, dear my dear.
The waiter, aged one hundred & nine, is
bringing me a hot, flat beer; that is, he
is shaking it over the carpet, and giving
me the empty glass.
To your health, my darling, & your beauty,
& your body, and our love for ever.

And all the things, too, in my life, now, involve you from head to foot. I wish your head were in my arms, as I sit mooning here, but I should be glad of your body, which I adore, were joined on to it. Smile secretly for me, as I, salted with loneliness, am smiling for you as I write: to the surprise of a pickled member: I mean, a man who looks pickled and who's reading *Punch* upside down in a doldrum. Smile for me, Pearl my true dear, wherever you read this. When your last letter came, I smuggled it around, under my coat, for hours, gloating, before I dare open it; no, not only gloating, for I was terrified too: perhaps you were dead, (though I would have known), or forgetful, or censorious, for I am always, my love, a little scared of you, which is only as it should be, I never really daring to dream that you could be fond of me as I am fond – good God, "fond" for what shakes my body and my world – of you, dear my dear.

The waiter, aged one hundred & nine, is bringing me a hot, flat beer: that is, he is shaking it over the carpet, and giving me the empty glass.

To your health, my darling, & your beauty, & your body, and our love for ever.

Do you still arrive in England on the fourth of September, or will the war stop you, or some other madness? If the dark leagues say, No, to you, I will declare war on America.
Shall I meet the boat train in London?

And where shall we stay, for we must be together all the time's that possible.

Shall I book a room in an hotel?
This club is for men only: if you can call men those bloodshot turnips talking balls with knife-ground accents and belching, into their pewtered gravy, stories about the famous men who snubbed them.

We must be together, oh every moment we can.
Tell me what to do, what you want to do.

Write soon, dear darling Pearl dear.

I kiss your heart.

Dylan

And I'll write again, next week. Always I imagine I have some wonderful news to tell you, and always it is the same news and new to you no longer. I love you.

2/

Do you still arrive in England on the fourth of September, or will the war stop you, or some other madness? If the dark leagues say, No, to you, I will declare war on America.

Shall I meet the boat train in London?

And where shall we stay, for we must be together all the time's that possible.

Shall I book a room in an hotel?

This club is for Men Only: if you can call men these bloodshot turnips talking balls with knife-ground accents and belching, into their pewtered gravy, stories about the famous men who snubbed them.

We must be together, oh every moment we can.

Tell me what to do, what you want to do.

Write soon, dear darling Pearl dear.

I kiss your heart.

Dylan

And I'll write again, next week. Always I imagine I have some wonderful news to tell you, and always it is the same news and new to you no longer. I love you.

Letter Three

August 13th 1950. [On three sheets of Savage Club notepaper]

I have suddenly found the first letter. Not
in a book at   all but wrapped i
a handkerchief   in the bottom of
a suitcase, and   send it with this,
all crumpled.

SAVAGE CLUB

TELEGRAMS:
"SAVAGE CLUB" LONDON.
TELEPHONE:
WHITEHALL 5264-5-6.

1, CARLTON HOUSE TERRACE.

LONDON. S. W. 1.

August 13 1950.

Pearl my very dear, my dear Pearl, just
an hour ago I opened your Pineapple
letters (the two typed ones), and in
the silence of my lonely room high
above the traffic's boom I read them
down to the lovely rind. I love you,
Pearl.

I wrote a letter last week, but
delayed sending it because I couldn't,
from yours, decipher if you lived at
nine or ninety one, and I couldn't
remember; though everything else about
your home I remember with my eyes,
and my body, and your body, and
my heart and — thank the lord — yours.
And I couldn't find the address of
Harper's Lupanar, and so I put the
letter in a book. And then I couldn't
remember which book; I looked in a
Blake, a Milton, a Wordsworth, a
W.W. Jacobs, even a thin, shrieking
Rothko, but my love to you wasn't in
any of them. Perhaps I double bluffed

I have suddenly found the first letter. Not in a book
at all but wrapped in a handkerchief at the bottom
of a suitcase. I send it with this, all crumpled.

August 13 1950.

Pearl my very dear, my dear Pearl, just an hour ago I
opened your Pineapple letters (the two typed ones),
and in the silence of my lonely room high above the
traffic's boom I read them down to the lovely rind. I
love you Pearl.

I wrote a letter last week, but delayed sending
it because I couldn't from yours, decipher if
you lived at nine or ninety one, and I couldn't
remember; though everything else about your
home I remember with my eyes, and my body, and
your body, and my heart and – thank the lord –
yours. And I couldn't find the address of Harper's
Rupanar, and so I put the letter in a book. And
then I couldn't remember which book; I looked in
a Blake, a Milton, a Wordsworth, a W. W. Jacobs,
even a thin, shrieking Roethke, but my love to you
wasn't in any of them. Perhaps I double bluffed

2/

and put it in an Oscar Tupper. And
I waited for something to happen —
this was in the gully country — but
nothing did and I came to London
and there were two letters, typed,
with ninety one clear as the moon
on them. I love you, Pearl.

When I find the first
letter, in Mrs Benton, wen pal Wilson,
the Collected Todd, Half Hours with
Jeremy Taylor, Engineering for Girls,
I'll post it on. The news will not
be dated, because there isn't any:
only the love, and want, and need,
of you.

The afternoon of (I nearly wrote
August, being so greedy) September
the third! Oh, my darling. Though
you must, you must, write me
before, you must, too, wire me, from
the travelling ship, or phone this
club from Southampton or wherever
you arrive, to say what time
your boat train will arrive in
London. And I'll be there to meet
it, small, red, fat, and in love.

My other letter asked,
and so must this: Where do you
stay in London? Where can I stay

2/

and put it in an Oscar Tupper. And I waited for something to happen – this was in the gully country – but nothing did and I came to London and there were two letters, typed, with ninety one clear as the moon on them. I love you, Pearl.

When I find the first letter in Mrs Beeton, wen pal Wilson, the Collected Todd, Half Hours with Jeremy Taylor, Engineering for Girls, I'll post it on. The news will not be dated, because there isn't any: only the love, and want, and need of you.

The afternoon of (I nearly wrote August, being so greedy) September the third! Oh, my darling. Though you must, you must, write me before, your must, too, wire me, from the travelling ship, or phone this club from Southampton or wherever you arrive, to say what time your boat train will arrive in London. And I'll be there to meet it, small, red, fat, and in love.

My other letter asked, and so must this: Where do you stay in London? Where can I stay with you?

SAVAGE CLUB

TELEGRAMS:
"SAVAGE CLUB" LONDON.
TELEPHONE
WHITEHALL 5284-5-6.

1. CARLTON HOUSE TERRACE,

LONDON. S.W. 1.

3/

with you? You know that I must stay
with you every moment that is possible,
don't you? Shall I try to get an
hotel room? Do you go straight,
with all your luggage, to your London
friends? I must be with you, and
you know, to your ~~dear~~ depth, why.

Last night, in my club for
no gentlemen, I dreamed of you, and
you were as beautiful as you are but
you were dressed up as a small
girl with bows in hair on shoes, &
we both laughed so much that I cried
on your breasts.

I have been in a terrible dejection
lately. I have been miserably,
sleeplessly, near suicidally, without
money. And I find I cannot work.
My home is a little balsen the
country, bugger its birds, has ceased
to charm. I want to write long, sad
poems but must instead give little,
bitty radio readings to pay the rent

3/

You know that I must stay with you every moment that is possible, don't you? Shall I try to get an hotel room? Do you go straight, with all your luggage, to your London friends? I must be with you, and you know, to your dear depth, why.

Last night, in my club for no gentlemen, I dreamed of you, and you were as beautiful as you are but you were dressed up as a small girl with bows in hair on shoes, & we both laughed so much that I cried on your breasts.

I have been in terrible dejection lately. I have been miserably, sleeplessly, near suicidally, without money. And I find I cannot work. My home is a little belsen, the country, bugger its birds, has ceased to charm, I want to write long, sad poems but must instead give little, bitty radio readings to pay the rent

and fail to pay the grocer, milkman,
coalman, schoolman, and, above all, the
village chemist who sells, drink as
well. I think I shall have to take a
job in London, for as long as you
will be here. But there isn't any
future for us; hold me now, in the
long, undying present, and let me hold
you.

Oh, but London is a beast. Sticky or
grey, or both. After eleven at
night, dodo dead. I drift disconsolate
through the dead streets, putting off
and ~~off my clean, high, remote or~~
broken room. Would to God that you
were allowed to stay here with me.
Then the room would be an ~~enormous~~ enormous
field, shadowed, full of flowers and
running brooks and bottoms and
bottles, where, till the first fissionary
gleam, we'd lie close, happy, and
half die.
But though I hate London so much,
with you, my dear dear my darling my
dear, it will be different I know.
We'll find in it places I never found,
or see them ~~through~~ new love till
they shudder and bob and sing
like ghosts on a treadmill.
                    We'll go deep and quiet, or
skim very noisy.
We'll go to Brighton too, where all

4/

and fail to pay the grocer, milkman, coalman, schoolman, and above all, the village chemist who sells drink as well. I think I shall have to take a job in London for as long as you will be here. But there isn't any future for us; hold me now, in the long, undying present, and let me hold you.

Oh, but London is a beast. Sticky or grey, or both. After eleven at night, dodo dead. I drift disconsolate through the dead streets, putting off and off my clean, high, remote and broken room. Would to God that you were allowed to stay here with me; then the room would be an enormous field, shadowed, full of flowers and running brooks and bottoms and bottles, where, till the first fissionary gleam, we'd lie close, happy, and half die.

But though I hate London so much, with you, my dear dear my darling my dear, it will be different I know. We'll find it in places I' never found, or see them through new love till they shudder and bob and sing like ghosts on a treadmill.
                        We'll go deep and quiet, or skim very noisy.

We'll go to Brighton too, where all

SAVAGE CLUB

TELEGRAMS:
"SAVAGE CLUB", LONDON
TELEPHONE:
WHITEHALL 5284 5-6

1. CARLTON HOUSE TERRACE,

LONDON. S. W. 1.

5/

naughty people go. I love you, Pearl.
        Slipper in. Lover me low.
Rub me in pearl. The stones woof.
Lower me, love. (A fragment by Ted.)
        My days are a row of
pottering puttings-off. I wait only for
you. I have written one radio feature, and
half a dirty poem. I have lectured
to half a dozen provincial Art's Societies,
indignant with maidenheads. I have
read Donne & Poe on the air. I have
looked at my comic half-finished novel and
screamed.

I have thought of you.

I hope to Christ this reaches you before
you sail. If it does not, my cable
will.

                    Forever,

                        Dylan.

5/

naughty people go. I love you, Pearl.

Slipper in. Lover me low. Rub me in pearl. The stones woof. Lower me, love. (A fragment by Ted.)

My days are a row of pottering puttings-off. I wait only for you. I have written one radio feature, and half a dirty poem. I have lectured to half a dozen provincial Arts societies indignant with maidenheads. I have read Donne & Poe on the air. I have looked at my comic half-finished novel and screamed.

I have thought of you.

I hope to Christ this reaches you before you sail. If it does not, my cable will.

Forever,

Dylan.

Letter Four

19th September 1950. Sent from The Boat House, Laugharne.

Boat House,
Laugharne,
Wales.

19 Sep 50

My Darling Pearl.

Just a very little note to say I love you.
I got back to find Caitlin unhurt, not indeed in
hospital at all. That information was just part
of the grey friend's service. But she was distressed.
I am coming, with Caitlin, to London on about
the 24 of this month. I will ring you. We will
meet, if you are still in London, so quietly
nobody shall see or hear us. Nobody. I would
have written as soon as I got back to Wales,
but my stomach (I don't want to shout that word)
was so galloping I just retired to a corner &
let it gallop. Also, I had to tell so many
lies, I was doubly sick. Forgive me, dear,
for all the pain I've made you by having -
haunting & hunting me, that grey scum. I love
you, dear, & hope to God this reaches you, & that
soon I reach you too.

Dylan.

Oh, what a snivelling note to you, my darling, when I
could write two Wars & Peaces. Believe in me. I'm nasty, but
I adore you. I wouldn't hurt you. Nothing is
impossible for us: it can't be. And out of everything
we'll make, somehow, some happiness together again &
again & again till the end of whatever.

But, still, I cannot forgive myself for not having
written so long before this. It is not for want
of thinking of you, my Pearl. Every moment I do, &
every hour.

Boat House
Laugharne
Wales
19 Sep 50

My Darling Pearl,

Just a very little note to say I love you.

I got back to find Caitlin unhurt, not indeed in hospital at all. That information was just part of the grey fiend's service. But she was distressed. I am coming, with Caitlin, to London on about the 24 of this month. I will ring you. We will meet, if you are still in London, so quietly nobody shall see or hear us. Nobody. I would have written as soon as I got back to Wales, but my stomach (I don't want to shout that word) was so galloping I just retired to a Corran & let it gallop. Also, I had to tell so many lies, I was doubly sick. Forgive me, dear, for all the pain I've made you by having, haunting & hurting me, that grey scum. I love you, dear, & hope to God this reaches you, & that soon I reach you too.

Dylan

Oh, what a snivelling note to you, my darling, when I could write two Wars & Peaces. Believe in me. I'm nasty, but I adore you. I wouldn't hurt you. Nothing is impossible for us: it can't be. And out of everything we'll make, somehow, some happiness together again & again & again till the end of whatever.

But, still, I cannot forgive myself for not having written so long before this. It is not for want of thinking of you, my Pearl. Every moment I do, of every hour.

Letter Five

December 20th, 1950. Sent from John Davenport's London address.

By. Air. Mail.

⑤

Dec 20 1950

Pearl Kazin,
Villa Fontana Vecchia,
Taormina,
Sicilia,
Italy

December 20. 1950.

Pearl my darling, my lost dear and I know who lost you but now I've found you, Pearl oh Pearl forgive me now, I love you. How can I tell you I love you so that you will believe me? If you were near me, I could tell you and you would have to believe me or I would put my finger in my navel and unwind myself, I would vanish through my ear and stretch out one arm from my ear to pull my bottom in, you would have to believe me because the truth would come crackling and screaming out of me and set your breasts and hair alight. Oh God, Pearl my darling dear. If only, if only. And all the seconds we were together, half of my heart, the half that wears a hat, was saying: Soon it will be over bang like that, you are happy but, I am happy but, you love Pearl but, O kiss her again but, but, but. But the naked half said: You shall love each other for ever, never forget, hold hard near and far. How did it happen? How did we pass each other blindly in some street? How did one shadow go under the sea, with the other rising all lost and seaweedy? We moved at the same time in two different dark Londons, weeping sleepwalkers. I love you, Pearl. The snow's falling on the sea beyond the window of this hut on a cliff where, in the half dark, I know you, I do know you, body and spirit beautifully all around and inside me, and I wish we could roll and yell. Love in the snow till the peeping Tom seapolicemen came. I love you.

as from
c/o John Davenport
4 Rossetti House,
Flood Street,
London S. W. 3.

December 20, 1950.

Pearl my darling, my lost dear and I know who lost you but now I've found you, Pearl oh Pearl forgive me now, I love you. How can I tell you I love you so that you will believe me? If you were near me, I could tell you and you would <u>have</u> to believe me or I would put my finger in my navel and unwind myself, I would vanish through my ear and stretch out one arm from my ear to pull my bottom in, you would <u>have</u> to believe me because the truth would come crackling and screaming out of me and set your breasts and hair alight. Oh God, Pearl my darling dear. If only, if only. And all the seconds we were together, half of my heart, the half that wears a hat, was saying: Soon it will be over bang like that, you are happy but, I am happy but, you love Pearl but, O kiss her again but, but, but. But the naked half said: You shall love each other for ever, never forget, hold hard near and far. How did it happen? How did we pass each other blindly in some street? How did one shadow go under the sea, with the other rising all lost and seaweedy? We moved at the same time in two different dark Londons, weeping sleepwalkers. I love you, Pearl. The snow's falling on the sea beyond the window of this hut on a cliff where, in the half dark, I know you, I do know you, body and spirit beautifully all around and inside me, and I wish we could roll and yell. Love in the snow till the peeping Tom seapoliceman came. I love you.

2

I came up to London when you were in France, and very soon fell ill. No letters were forwarded to me from the Savage Club. I mean, no letters from you. And this was not surprising, for, as I discovered this week, the grey lady had, when I was ill, called each morning to "collect my letters" for me; it was very kind of her, the porters said. And any letters of yours she destroyed, or hid among her snakes, or framed in her sewer, or sucked up like a hoover into her worms, or celebrated her grey mass before. Whatever she did with them, they are gone. And I never saw one lovely line. And then my pleurisy turned into pneumonia — I had slept, outside in the rain one night — and I didn't know anything. You cried in the fever as though I were dead. And then I was brought back here, to the sea, to recover, and then two Sicilian letters came. Oh, darling Pearl. In your lost lonliness, my silence every day must been such a treachery as there never was before. I know that I shall always love you, that I have never deserted you, and that we shall be together. I've lived in a lost lonliness, too; I didn't know where you were; there wasn't any meaning in the world going round, in the snow-flocks, in the wakings and drownings, in the smoke of words, what was I here for, what was I doing, something had gone wrong in the original light, and the spirit was as spiritual as a moustache-cup. I didn't know what I was meant to do. Should I lie down foaming or throw my head out to the rooks or whisper your name in the secret w.c.'s of the night or write a sonnet to a mouse or join the womens' Land Army or cut my throat with a bucket or sit down in the garden and grow leaves? A terrible doctor had come

2/

       I came up to London when you were in France, and very soon fell ill. No letters were forwarded to me from the Savage Club. I mean, no letters from you. And this was not surprising, for, as I discovered this week, the grey lady had, when I was ill, called each morning to "collect my letters for me." It was very kind of her, the porters said. And any letters of yours she destroyed, or hid among her snakes, or framed in her sewer, or sucked up like a hoover into her worms, or celebrated her grey mass before. Whatever she did with them, they are gone. And I never saw one lovely line. And then my pleurisy turned into pneumonia – I had slept outside in the rain one night – and I didn't know anything. You cried in the fever as though I were dead. And then I was brought back here, to the sea, to recover, and then two Sicilian letters came. Oh, darling Pearl. In your lost loneliness, my silence every day must been such a treachery as there never was before. I know that I shall always love you, that I have never deserted you, and that we shall be together. I've lived in lost loneliness, too; I didn't know where you were; there wasn't any meaning in the world going round, in the snow-flocks, in the wakings and drownings, in the smoke of words, what was I here for, what was I doing, something had gone wrong in the original light, and the spirit was as spiritual as a moustache-cup. I didn't know what I was meant to do. Should I lie down foaming or throw my head out to the rooks or whisper your name in the secret w.c.'s of the night or write a sonnet to a mouse or join the Women's Land Army or cut my throat with a bucket or sit down in the garden and grow leaves? A terrible doctor had come

when I was ill, and extracted my cause. I looked
in the looking-glass and saw two nipples with
heavy eyebrows like Frank Harris's. I squinted
into graveyard bedrooms like a voyeur zombie.
I wrote War and Peace, quickly, and translated
a concerto into welsh. What was I up to
this day of disgrace, masturbating in a
straitjacket? I read the newspapers carefully,
working out assassination plots in code.
Strangers disguised as myself called
regularly at the trap door, demanding
subscriptions for obscene organisations,
making me sign petitions to the king to
prohibit breathing. All the food I ate
tasted of the Pope. There was I, knowing you
were dead, knowing you were dust, knowing
you had never existed. Oh, Pearl, Pearl,
whom I love & want, I was ill in the wards
of the world, but now the snow's all suns.
And now I'm well because I know where you
are, even if you have moved from where you
were, and because I know, my dear, that
our love is alive. I'm well, and can work,
and soon we will meet, somehow, if only
for one prodigiously dear day and night. "Now
I can work". Oh, Christ above, and I know, too,
what that means. Next week, in order to make
money, I am to go to Persia to write a
filmscript for the Anglo-Iranian Oil Company.
I shall love you in Shiraz and Isfahan and
Persepolis and even in Abadan. I shall love
you from the oily Gulf to the Caspian Sea. It
does not matter now, so deeply much, that we
shall not meet for a short or a long time,
because our love is alive and we can wait.
I shall be back in London in the middle of
February. I shall write you to from Persia.
Please, my sweet, write to me at the Davenport
address: I have no fixed Persian address, &
the Savage I will never trust again. I kiss your
heart. Tell me where you will be in middle February.
I kiss you everywhere!

Dylan.

3/

when I was ill, and extracted my cause. I looked in the looking-glass and saw two nipples with heavy eyebrows like Frank Harris's. I squinted into graveyard bedrooms like a voyeur zombie. I wrote *War and Peace*, quickly, and translated a concerto into Welsh. What was I up to this day of disgrace, masturbating in a straightjacket? I read the newspapers carefully, working out assassination plots in code. Strangers disguised as myself called regularly at the trap door, demanding subscriptions for obscene organisations, making me sign petitions to the King to prohibit breathing. All the food I ate tasted of the Pope. Where was I, knowing you were dead, knowing you were dust, knowing you had never existed. Oh, Pearl, Pearl whom I love & want. I was ill in the wards of the world, but now the snow's all suns. And now I'm well because I know where you are, even if you have moved from where you were, and because I know, my dear, that our love is alive. I'm well, and can work and soon we will meet, somehow, if only for one prodigiously dear day and night. "Now I can work." Oh Christ above, and I know too, what that means. Next week, in order to make money, I am to go to Persia to write a filmscript for the Anglo-Iranian Oil Company. I shall love you in Shiraz and Isfahan and Persepolis and even in Abadan. I shall love you from the oilly Gulf to the Caspian Sea. It does not matter now, so deeply much, that we shall not meet for a short or a long time, because our love is alive and we can wait. I shall be back in London in the middle of February. I shall write you to from Persia. Please, my sweet, write to me at the Davenport address: I have no fixed Persian address, & the Savage I will never trust again. I kiss your heart. Tell me where you will be in middle February. I kiss you everywhere.

Dylan.

Letter Six

February 1951. Sent from Persia.

Abadan

Pearl:
I am writing this in a tasty, stiff-lipped, liverish, British Guest House in puking Abadan on, as you bloody well know, the foul blue boiling Persian buggering Gulf. And lost God blast, I gasp between gassed vodkas, all crude and cruel fuel oil, all petroleum under frying heaven, benzole, bitumen, bunkers and tankers, pipes and refineries, wells and derricks, gushers and super-fractionators and Shatt-el-Arab and all. Today I was taken to see a great new black-tower hissing and coiling monster just erected in the middle of the refinery. It cost eight million pounds. It is called a Cat-Cracker.

Abadan is inhibited almost entirely by British — or so it seems. There are thousands of young Britishers in the bachelor quarters, all quietly seething. Many snap in the heat of their ingrowing sex and the sun, and are sent back, baying, to Britain. Immediately, their places are taken by fresh recruits: young, well-groomed pups with fair moustaches and bristling pipes, who, in the soaking summer, soon age, go bristled about, chainsmoke damp hanging fags, scream blue on arak, toss themselves, trembly all sleepless night in the toss-trembling bachelors quarters, answer the three-knock knock at the midnight door, see before them in the hot moonlight a wetmouthed Persian girls from the bazaar who asks, by custom, for a glass of water, invites the girls in, blushes, stammers, gropes, are lost. These old-young men are shipped back also, packed full with shame and penicillin. And the more cautious stay on, boozed, shrill, hunted red-eyed, damp-palmed, wog-hating, hysterically remembering gay wonderful London so white-skinned & willing.

I visited oil-fields in the mountains last week. By night, the noise of frustrated geologists howled louder than the jackals outside my tent. Utterly damned, the dishonourable, craven, knowledgeable, self-pitying jackals screamed & wailed in the abysses of their guilt and the stinking garbage pails. "Rosemary", "Jennifer", "Margery", "Pearl" cried the near-male unsleepers in their near-sleep. And the hyenas laughed like billyho deep down in their dark, diseased throats.

Abadan

Pearl:

I am writing this in a tasty, stifflipped, liverish, British Guest House in puking Abadan, on, as you bloody well know, the foul blue boiling Persian buggering Gulf. And lost God blast, I gasp between gassed vodkas, all crude and cruel fuel oil, all petroleum under frying heaven, benzola, bitumen, bunkers and tankers, pipes and refineries, wells and derricks, gushers and super-fractionators and Shatt-el-Arab and all. Today I was taken to see a great new black-towered hissing and coiling monster just erected in the middle of the refinery. It cost eight million ponds. It is called a Cat-Cracker.

Abadan is inhibited almost entirely by British – or so it seems. There are thousands of young Britishers in the bachelor quarters, all quietly seething. Many snap in the heat of their ingrowing sex and the sun, and are sent back, baying, to Britain. Immediately, their places are taken by fresh recruits: young, wellgroomed pups with fair moustaches and briar pipes, who in the soaking summer, soon age, go bristled about, chainsmoke damp hanging fags, scream blue on arak, toss themselves trembly all sleepless night in the toss-trembling bachelors quarters, answer the three-knock knock at the midnight door, see before them in the hot moonlight wetmouthed Persian girls from the bazaar who ask, by custom, for a glass of water, invite the girls in, blush, stammer , grope, are lost. These old-young men are shipped back also, packed full with shame and penicillin. And the more cautious stay on, boozed, shrill, hunted, red-eyed, damp-palmed, wog-hating, hysterically remembering gay wonderful London so white-skinned & willing.

I visited oil-fields in the mountains last week. By night, the noise of frustrated geologists howled louder than the jackals outside my tent. Utterly damned, the dishonourable, craven, knowledgeable, self-pitying jackals screamed & wailed in the abysses of their guilt and the stinking garbage pails. "Rosemary", "Jennifer", "Margery", "Pearl", cried the near-male unsleepers in their near-sleep. And the hyenas laughed like billyho deep down in their dank, diseased throats.

O evergreen, gardened, cypressed, cinema'd, oil-tanked boulevarded, incense-and-armpit cradle of Persian culture, rock me soft before lorn hotel-bedtime, I have nostalgia and govt. My heart bears out for my Brooklyn love, and my toe pulses like a painful cucumber in the arraky bar. O city of Haffiz and Sadi, and mrs Wiltshire the Consul's wife, tickle me till my balloon toe dies and I drift towards Sicily. It was beautiful, indeed, to hear from you, to hear you in your letter, to know that, though thousands of miles apart, we are still together. Forget that cancerous woman and, if we can, all the dumb dark that lay between us for so long, Pearl my darling dear. I'll let you know when I return to England: some time at the end of February or early March, I think. Oh, we must, if you are still European and love. Goodnight, for a while (though only in one way) to bed, to dream. A lonely cold country, I'm going, mazed, stricken Persia, mosque and blindness, fountains & running sore, mudhuts, cadillac and pomegranate & Cat-Cracker, Beer in an hotel bar costs ten shillings a bottle; whiskey, one pound a nip. There is no night-life. Shiraz sleeps at nine. Then, through the dark, the low camel bells ring; jackals confess their unworthiness to live in an ignoble fury of siren howls, and utter their base and gutter-breath'd gratitude to the night that hides their abominable faces; insomniac dogs rumpus in the mountain villages, the Egyptian deputy-minister of Education, who has the next hotel room, drunkenly galumphs with a thin, hairy secretary, dervishes plead under my bed. There are wolves not far away. There is no night life here: The moon does what she does, vermin persist, camels sail, dogs defy, frogs gloat, snow-leopards drift, ibex do what they do, moufflon are peculiar, gazelles are lonely, donkeys are Christian, bears in the high hills hug. I wish you were here. All my love, Pearl sweetheart, and I will write before I leave here. I kiss your heart, and all of you. Dylan

2/   Shiraz

O evergreen, gardened, cypressed, cinema'd, oil-tanked Boulevarded, incense-and-armpit cradle of Persian culture, rock me soft before lorn hotel-bedtime, I have nostalgia and gout. My heart beats out for my Brooklyn love, and my toe pulses like a painful cucumber in the arraky bar. O city of Haffiz and Sad'i and Mrs Wiltshire the Consul's wife, tickle me till my balloon toe dies and I drift towards Sicily. It was beautiful, indeed to hear from you, to hear you in your letter, to know that, though thousands of miles apart, we are still together. Forget that cancerous woman and, if we can, all the dumb dark that lay between us for so long, Pearl my darling dear. I'll let you know when I return to England: some time at the end of February or early March, I think. Oh, we must, if you are still European meet somewhere then, and lie (though only in one way) and love. Goodnight, for a while, I'm going, mazed, to cold bed, to dream. A lonely country. And so is stricken Persia, mosque and blindness, fountains & mudhuts, cadillac and running sore, pomegranate & Cat-Cracker. Beer in a hotel bar costs ten shillings a bottle; whiskey, one pound a nip. There is no night-life. Shiraz sleeps at nine. Then, through the dark, the low camel bells ring, jackals confess their unworthiness to live in an ignoble fury of siren howls, and utter their base and gutter-breath'd gratitude to the night that hides their abominable faces; insomniac dogs rumpus in the mountain villages; the Egyptian deputy-minister of Education, who has the next hotel room, drunkenly gallumphs with a thin, hairy secretary; dervishes plead under my bed; there are wolves not far away. There is no night life here: The moon does what she does, vermin persist, camels sail, dogs defy, frogs gloat, snow-leopards drift, ibex do what they do, moufflon are peculiar, gazelles are lonely, donkeys are Christian, bears in the high hills hug. I wish you were here. All my love, Pearl sweetheart, and I will write before I leave here. I kiss your heart, and Dylan all of you.

A Note on the Letters

I have been pursuing and dealing in the books, manuscripts, letters, iconography and ephemera surrounding Dylan Thomas from my bookstore in his home town of Swansea for over forty years. In that time I have been fortunate in handling some quite remarkable materials – original letters to his wife, his family his friends; books inscribed to fellow writers and close friends and even the book he inscribed and gave to Charlie Chaplin when they met in Hollywood; sketches and doodles, the only known coloured gouache surrealist painting by him, and original photographs and portraits. I was lucky in that when I arrived in Swansea many of his close friends were still about. Vernon Watkins had died in America but his widow, the remarkable Gwen Watkins, became, and still is, a close friend, and she has been the source of much wonderful stuff, although her endless edifying conversations are what I treasure the most. I became friends with, and bought materials from, Dylan's close friends Mervyn Levy, Alfred Janes and Charles Fisher, and I handled the serious archives of Wynford Vaughan Thomas and Daniel Jones.

But I was also very well supported by my friends in the booktrade in the UK, in Europe and most especially by my American colleagues – they were all quick to offer me unusual items that came their way, but were also often very altruistic in pointing me towards collections and auctions containing remarkable items. And the Dylan–Pearl letters published here came to me via two very different but great English booksellers.

I first heard of this group of letters from Arthur Freeman, a London-based American, a scholarly Shakespeare expert and bibliogenius, late of Quaritch, but now gently trading as Arthur Freeman Rare Books, a leading London Antiquarian booksellers – he describes his approach to business now as being, 'laid back, to say the least – no advertising, no catalogues – like a call girl with an unlisted number, you might say.'

From that you might gather that Arthur is a poet and writer too. In fact a poem of his, accompanied by a portrait photograph of him by Dylan's American photographer friend Rollie McKenna, is included in an anthology of poetry compiled and edited by Bill Read and his partner John Malcolm Brinnin,* who figures large in this book. Bill Read went on to produce an early pictorial biography of Dylan – *The Days of Dylan Thomas* (1964).

This goes some way to explaining Arthur's connections with Dylan Thomas. Some three decades ago Arthur approached me at a book fair in Los Angeles, where I had a booth; he had a large and obviously Californian gent in tow. We were introduced – he was the owner of the Dylan–Pearl letters. A film executive at some high rank, he had been behind some pulp horror movies – *The Thing from the Swamp* or some such. He had decided to collect, and bought the letters on the understanding that they were to remain unpublished and unpublicised during the lifetime of the recipient. We spoke

---

*   Brinnin and Read, *The Modern Poets, An American–British Anthology*, 1963.

of Dylan Thomas in New York and around America and I tactfully indicated that should he ever wish to dispose of his treasure then… I gave him my business card and that was that.

Fast-forward a couple of swift decades and by then the current top London bookseller was Simon Finch, a youngish (by bookseller standards), very trendy, private-school-educated, colourful and lively cove. Simon had incredible taste and style in all things including rare books. And he had big cojones. He had opened a classy, tall, thin, rare-book-stuffed edifice off Bond Street and another amazing book shop in Notting Hill, the like of which had never been seen; white and grey and well-lit with shelves that looked like they had been designed by Gaudi; on opening night the window display featured Dennis Hopper's denim jacket worn in *Easy Rider* draped over the corner of the leather binding of a sixteenth century black-letter Chaucer. I had known Simon from his university days in Bristol where he had begun to deal in rare books and we had often done some business together, and I got vicarious pleasure observing his steady climb up the bookseller rankings.

Around the millenium, and quite out of the blue, Simon rang me – he was being offered the Dylan–Pearl letters, they were fantastic and would I like to go half-shares in the deal – the price quoted would have bought a half-share in a small terraced house in Swansea. Of course I would. I would go to London ASAP to read the letters and make the final deal. So a few days later I found myself upstairs in Simon's surreal Gaudiesque book cavern watched over by erotic images by Larry Clark, reading wonderful, innocent, charming love letters from a Welsh poet to his new love, a New York journalist. Simon breezed in, distracted and jumpy: he had a new girlfriend in L.A., and he wanted to move there, and he had the chance to buy a shack on a canal in Venice Beach and I had to buy the letters outright, and I had just days to pay else he would lose his love-nest and perhaps even his new friend!

We did the deal. I now owned the letters.

They came in a very ordinary royal blue folder with transparent pockets holding the originals; with both sides of the correspondence surrounding the original sale/purchase of the letters between a leading American rare bookselling firm in Chicago – Hammel and Barker and Mrs Daniel Bell – Pearl. Mrs Bell first offered some or all of the letters in 1970 but then she the had second thoughts and kept withdrawing the letters. She finally sold them in 1973, but even then she prevaricated, writing to Frances Hammel:

> This is an unforgivable thing to do to you I know but my
> conscience won't let me cash your check, and I hope it's
> not to late to call the whole thing off.

This brought a swift, well-reasoned and persuasive response from Hammel which clinched the sale.

The letters themselves are all you would expect of letters from a romantic young poet in his prime to a distant new younger lover – passionate, wordy, witty and poignant.

Opposite: Pearl's final moment of self-doubt;
and following page: Hammil & Barker's final
successful persuasive pitch.

February 20, 1973

Dear Miss Hammel,

This is an unforgivable thing to do to you, I know,
but my conscience won't let me cash your check, and I hope
it's not too late to call the whole thing off. I've been
feeling like a ghoul since your check arrived, and the feeling is ~~xx~~ intolerable.~~xxxxxxxx~~ I'm sorry I've caused you
all this trouble for nothing, and hope you will be able to
accept my apology.

Yours sincerely,

Pearl Bell

February 22, 1973

Dear Mrs. Bell,

What can I say that might let you change your feeling and be comfortable about doing so? I feel strongly that any important original material that adds to the understanding and knowledge of an author or artist should be preserved properly for future study. Our experience has been that an institution or dedicated collector who is willing to pay for what adds to the stature of the collection is serious and will preserve it, ensuring that it will eventually be used in an intelligent manner. If it is a gift, it may or may not be cared for. I'll give one example: When we approached Leonard Woolf about selling his wife's manuscripts and diaries, he said he had no need of the money and had planned to give them to the Bodleian. However, he discovered that the one manuscript he had given when Virginia Woolf died couldn't be found in the Library. He ended by letting us place the lot with restriction in the New York Public Library for a very respectable sum. This material now forms a nucleus of letters and manuscripts of the period that can be and are used by interested scholars.

It comes down to your receiving money that insures the preservation of Dylan Thomas's letters; we, as intermediaries, get a commission for placing them properly. I feel sure the money isn't the important thing with either of us, and I don't believe it should bother your conscience or make you feel like a ghoul.

While we have already felt out a library as to their interest (without giving details) and had a promising reaction, we do not wish to make you so unhappy. Please think it over and let me know.

Afterword: A Life of Pearl Kazin Bell by David Bell

Pearl Kazin Bell was born on October 12th, 1922, in Brooklyn, New York. She was the daughter of Jewish immigrants from the Russian Empire. Her father, Gedaliah Kazin (known as Charles or Charlie in the US) immigrated sometime around 1908. His family name was originally Kozinitch, and he most likely came from the small shtetl of this name, which was located in the Jewish Pale of Settlement in the Russian Empire, north of Minsk. Gedaliah was trained as a farmer at a Baron de Hirsch school in Russia, and in the US travelled for several years, and was even employed on a ranch in Wyoming, but finally returned to New York City where he became a house painter. He married Gita Faigelman, also known as 'Gussie', who also immigrated from the Russian Empire, in her case from a town called Dokhshitsy, between Minsk and Vilna. She worked in the US as a dressmaker, making 'knock-offs' of current fashions for private customers. Pearl's parents were married in 1914, and had their first child, Alfred, in 1915. Alfred grew up to become a notable American literary figure, the author of *On Native Grounds*, *A Walker in the City*, *New York Jew*, and much else.

Pearl grew up in the section of Brooklyn called Brownsville, a poor neighbourhood then largely inhabited by Jewish immigrants.

Her family was not particularly observant of the Jewish religion, and her father was a socialist. Pearl's first language was Yiddish, although she quickly learned English in the streets and in school. However, as a child she attended a socialist Sunday school, in which she learned to read and write in Yiddish, and all her life she could speak a very elegant, literary Yiddish. During the Great Depression the family was very poor.

Pearl attended Franklin K. Lane High School in Brooklyn, graduating in 1938. She was very briefly a member of the Young Communist League while in high school. From 1938 to 1942 she attended Brooklyn College, a free public college, graduating with a degree in English. She was then admitted to graduate programs at Radcliffe College, the then-sister school of Harvard University. She studied there for two years, working in particular with the renowned scholar F. O. Matthiessen. At Radcliffe, she took elocution classes to lose her strong Brooklyn accent, and was quite homesick for New York City. In 1944, she decided to leave Radcliffe, in part because, thanks to wartime conditions, as a woman she had a better chance of getting a job in journalism in New York City.

Back in New York, she briefly worked for *Time Magazine* as a researcher, and then moved to *Harper's Bazaar*. There, she worked with the literary editor Mary Louise Aswell, a Philadelphia Quaker who treated her as something of an adoptive daughter ('Mary Lou' was also my godmother). It was while at *Harper's Bazaar* that my mother had the relationship with Dylan Thomas. In the summer of 1949 (I think) Pearl also spent time at the Yaddo Writers' Workshop in upstate New York where she met and became friends with the poet Elizabeth Bishop.

After the end of the affair with Dylan Thomas, Pearl was married, in August of 1951, to Victor Kraft, a photographer then working in Brazil, who had previously been the lover of the composer Aaron Copland. Pearl moved to Brazil to be with Kraft, but the marriage was very short-lived. After leaving Kraft in 1952, Pearl stayed on for some time in Brazil herself, but then returned to New York. A year or two later, she went to Europe, where she spent time by herself, writing, in Spain, and also some time visiting her friend Truman Capote in Sicily. By 1954, however, she was back in New York City, where she became a copy editor on *The New Yorker* magazine. She published a story in *The New Yorker*, about her immigrant family and the Thanksgiving holiday, in 1954.

Pearl remained in New York throughout the 1950s. She dated my father, Daniel Bell, briefly in 1956-7, broke off with him, and for a time also dated the young actor William Shatner, later of *Star Trek* fame. Her mother died of cancer in 1958. In 1959 she began to date my father again. They were married in December of 1960. I was born in November of 1961, and around this time my mother stopped working at *The New Yorker*. I am her only child.

Our family continued to live in New York until 1970, which is also the year Pearl's father died. My father was Professor of Sociology at Columbia, and we lived in university apartments on Riverside Drive in Manhattan. In the late 1960s, my mother taught Expository Writing at Columbia. Summers were spent on Martha's Vineyard island off the coast of Massachusetts, where my parents had a house built in 1966. They spent nearly every summer there until 2002. In 1976–77 we lived in London, and in 1987–88 my parents lived in Cambridge, England.

In 1970 my father was hired by Harvard University, and the family moved to Cambridge, Massachusetts. In the early 1970s my mother began working as the regular fiction critic for *The New Leader*, a weekly political and literary magazine published by Ladies Garment Workers' Union, and a publication with which my father and uncle Alfred Kazin had long-standing connections. After a few years, she moved over to become the fiction critic for *Commentary*, the monthly magazine of the American Jewish Committee, and an influential political and literary publication. She stopped writing for *Commentary* in the early 1980s when it became too conservative for her tastes, and she began writing for the long-standing intellectual quarterly *Partisan Review*. She also reviewed regularly at this point for *The New Republic* and *The Wall Street Journal*. She wrote a novel, but never attempted to publish it. She also collected her essays and reviews on women's fiction, but did not find a publisher. In the 1990s my father had many health difficulties, and much of my mother's time was taken up caring for him.

In 2002, at the age of 79, my mother had a catastrophic fall on the stairs at a friend's house in Boston. She suffered severe brain damage, and spent many weeks in a coma. She then spent several more weeks in rehabilitation, but was left unable to walk, or to use one arm, and her cognitive functions were severely impaired. She could recognize people, but not follow a conversation, or read, or speak normally. She spent time in a series of nursing homes until my father moved her back to their home in Cambridge with 24-hour nursing care. Her condition slowly declined, and by 2008 she could no longer speak. After my father's death in January, 2011, I moved her to a Jewish nursing home near my own home in Princeton, NJ. In June of 2011, after a bad bout of pneumonia, she died there, aged 88. She is buried in the Jewish Cemetery on Martha's Vineyard, next to my father.

My mother is mentioned in many journals and published correspondences of literary figures from the late 1940s and 1950s, in particular relating to her relationship with Dylan Thomas. She is not mentioned in her brother's autobiographical works, although she does appear sporadically in his published journals. She is mentioned as well in the memoir of Alfred's third wife Ann Birstein. Among her publications are the early stories in *Botteghe Oscure* and *The New Yorker*, an essay about Elizabeth Bishop for *Partisan Review*, an autobiographical essay about her time at Radcliffe for *The American Scholar*, and also her voluminous book reviews. I have a small collection of letters that she sent to her friend Beatrice Hofstadter White in the 1950s, but few other letters.

BOTTEGHE OSCVRE

An International Review of New Literature

Since 1948 BOTTEGHE OSCURE (pronounced BO-TAY-GAY OS-COO-RAY) has been published twice a year in Rome, in the Via delle Botteghe Oscure, the *Street of the Dark Shops*, so-called from shops established during the Middle Ages in the ruined Roman arcades.

Edited by an American-born Italian Princess, BOTTEGHE OSCURE has an unique place in American publishing. It is devoted to printing the latest work of world-famous writers alongside the new voices who are forming the reading tastes of tomorrow.

Almost a literary tradition in itself, BOTTEGHE OSCURE offers in each issue 500 beautifully printed pages of new and important American, English, Italian and French writing. This review sets new standards, embraces all new trends in American writing

Appendix: *The Jester* by Pearl Kazin
*One further curious synchronicity –

Pearl Kazin was a writer and critic. She spent time at the influential Yaddo Writing Retreat in upstate New York and was a close friend with the poet Elizabeth Bishop and with Truman Capote. She published stories in the *New Yorker* and for many years was the the literary critic for the *New Leader* magazine before joining the staff of *Commentary*. However, an early short story of Pearl's, *The Jester*, was published in the upmarket multi-lingual Italian literary magazine *Botteghe Oscure*, which was based in Rome [the title translates as the *Street of the Dark Shops*]. The magazine was a unique creation of its editor and patron Marguerite Caetani, an American-born Italian Princess. The periodical's published aim was to print 'the latest work of world-famous writers alongside the new voices who are forming the reading tastes of tomorrow'.

In Issue IX of this hefty book-sized offering, printed on fine paper in elegant fonts and published in 1952, the leading 'world-famous' writer Dylan Thomas' most famous work *Under Milk Wood* is published here for the very first time as *Llareggub – A Piece for Radio Perhaps*. And by a curious syncronicity one of the 'new voices' is Pearl Kazin, whose story of a New York literary eccentric brings Dylan and Pearl together again, albeit only upon the pages of the same publication. Some critics have tried to see something of Dylan Thomas in Pearl's character 'Kuney', the anti-hero in her story.

BOTTEGHE OSCVRE

INTERNATIONAL REVIEW OF NEW LITERATUR

Unpublished works by the most important and vital writers in prose and poetry of our time. Issued in Spring and Autumn.

IX

The Jester
Pearl Kazin

It is odd that I think of Kuney so much in link with the seasons. When his memory absorbs me now, I turn with strange formality to the extremes of the earth's turning. The summer of his death, New York was a blazing, sputtering beast. The heat, beginning late in May, had swelled without break in a gluttonous rage for sacrifice. It wasted no minutes, and each morning I would wake out of a sweating, steaming sleep, my dreams dissolved in my own dampness, my eyes twitching with fear of the sun. It was a summer that made me loathe daylight, and I deplored in a dulled lamentation the length which summer gives to the sun's light. I walked stupidly through the deadened glare of each day, feeling nothing but heat and my fear of the burning, stifling brightness, ticking off the hours till darkness. But night brought little relief to a sullen city which gasped for breath so violently, the sick rhythm could be felt and heard as a monstrous spasm. Everyone who could took flight. Everyone suddenly remembered the usually scorned, dull friends who had taken cottages in Easthampton and Fire Island and even the mosquito-ridden lakes of New Jersey, and fled to the cooling water. Each day the newspapers ran the familiar photographs of a million buttocks sprawling in slovenly, thick discomfort on the beaches, and the headlines grimly counted the thousands who churned up the water that islands the parts of New York. Terrible quarrels broke out constantly among strangers on the subways, and the slightest touch between steaming neighbours in the rush hours became sufficient cause for murder.

Yet it was Kuney among us all, who died of the city's excess that summer. He, who adored New York and hailed its every season with brazen hallelujahs, was destroyed by it. For he loved to think of himself as the supreme manufactured urban man. All cities can become mechanical tyrants, plaguing their inhabitants without mercy, but Kuney accepted the perversities of New York with a lusty pleasure in its unfeeling wantonness. He never took refuge in country weekends, and he loved to boast, eyebrows raised in seeming wonder at his listener's disbelief, that he had never abandoned his beloved cement, and no one could remember ever having seen him on a beach.

Kuney was a fat man, the kind who takes refuge in laughing at his own grossness, but the slight edge of desperation that always cut into his jokes about his size often lessened the protection of his mockery. For his devotion to the city, no matter how its seasons might oppress others, kept him from needing to expose his absurd and impossible nakedness. He often boasted that on days when New York had been drained of its noisy, clicking millions, and the great geometric jungles of Wall Street and Union Square and Seventh Avenue stood hollow and bereft in the hot weekend sun, he found his pleasure in walking happily through the streets, taking on the burden of those who had left these wonders to silence, shocked at all the arrested energy of silent elevators, typewriters, adding machines and telephones, humming his solitary hosanna to the inhuman and silent desert of brick and steel and glass which, in its mad permanence on such a day, enclosed nothing but himself and was created, as it seemed, only for him, who worshipped it. There it stood, this marvel of a great city, ruinous to some perhaps, in its oppressive mass of place and structure, with only his dedicated presence to give it tribute. At such moments Kuney could be happiest – he could truly think himself king and father of all he saw.

Summer was the time of Kuney's death, but I think too of the other seasons when he had made his unique exultant sacrifices to the city. An escapade of his in the year before he died became one of his favourite boasts, and he told the story often, with the same giggling half-pride in his heroism. He alone, he claimed, had roamed unflinching through the crippled city in a great blizzard that assaulted New York shortly before Christmas. For more than twelve hours, he said – and I knew he spoke the truth, for such wildly useless adventures were actually sober rituals to him, in his praise of being urban – the city took on a new perspective, became his very own to rediscover and possess. Each clogged and desolate street corner, every choked crossing, every curb and hydrant softened by the snow, became a hurdle he happily trudged around and across in his black Arctics and vast black overcoat. Somehow, as he told it, it seemed that he had made less dangerous with his presence the damage that was falling with the snow. And the purposeless bravado of his adventure took its toll.

In his illness afterwards, he held sniffling and bellowing court from his bed, surrounded by a holiday of martyrdom that he wanted his friends to come and share. What wonderfully wicked weather, and hadn't he saved New York, he roared out, in sometime ridicule of the pose he struck, hadn't he been the only one willing to take his chances while the rest of us, cowards all, crouched inside our locked, safe windows and watched the drifts mount and move outside? I applauded and howled with the others who had come to pay him mocking homage for his senseless safari through the snow, taking our own giddy vengeance on both the city and my friend by coming to hear out and praise and laugh at his absurd extravagance.

I was there. So too were ten more of his friends. I never could remember afterwards exactly how many had appeared in the course of a 'Kuney party'. Whether he was sick or healthy, idle or claiming work, someone was always at Kuney's side to keep him unalone – someone who had always just dropped in, was merely passing, could stay for only a minute. But someone was always there, drawn by undecipherable temptations, to protect Kuney from his solitude. He was alone when he died: that was the one time. If he feared that a chance route or idle walk might lead no one to his home, he would, in a steady series of phone calls, badger the lonely ones, the idle ones, the bored, endless ranks in search of distraction who are always ready to go anywhere in New York, to be saved from themselves. He could always rout out the many who, with desperate excuses to themselves, obeyed Kuney's taunting command. And I, on that winter afternoon, was one of the chosen, reluctantly obedient, ready to help him fend off the goblins of the surrounded self.

'Come in, come in!'

He cried out to each newcomer: 'How wonderful! How lovely to see you,' flapping his hands in sham surprise at encountering each visitor, as though it were all quite accidental that they should be there, with him, all the 'right ones' together. 'Sit down, you have to sit down immediately and hear all about my divine day. Now don't dawdle!' His fingers played frantically with his beard, a flamboyant joke of two years back which he had kept, and he loved to tell how he had acquired a beard when he had been taking 'just millions and millions of folders full of notes' for a book about Lucrezia Borgia, and which he had then abandoned when, as he explained, 'it turned into a novel, right in my hands, as though I were some awful Pygmalion. And what could I do then? A novel – my God! – it would just have to be Proust, pure Proust...and all that gossip. Oh, you know, it would just have drowned me. Not that I didn't have enough material...'

Smothering his visitors in a blanket of loud and extravagant hellos, he shrieked his salutes and commands and questions in wild disconnection, sent each of us with mocking authority to the different chairs he wanted us to take, arranging us all in a muddled frieze that solaced him with its makeshift variety as he lay there. And the stream of gossip, of warning, of affectionate reproach ran ceaselessly from him. With me, he had a special by-play, embraces and taunts for the favoured, and I was snared in a nervous tangle of arms and face and beard and distracted chatter, caught in the pleasure of company.

For I knew this then, and better now: in the wild indiscretion through which he exposed himself to any easy, laughing scorn, he helped me disguise and forget myself for a few hours. I am tempted, when I think of this, to call Kuney a poor lamb, to moan at the way he wasted himself, threw himself away so lavishly and incessantly as he kicked over all the fences of privacy. Always available, he made his most intimate friends share him with thousands of strangers who ebbed and receded through his life with the indiscriminate regularity of the tides. If he let himself be shared with less than the world, as he perhaps knew, he might have nothing at all to give, to anything or anyone. His telephone was thus: always busy, perched at his side or held in his pudgy fingers like a pampered black cat.

But now, trying to see him with the tranquil steady gaze I never had for him before his death, I must not sneer at how prodigally he spent himself, for surely the generosity was meant. And though I might pretend to innocence, I remember with pain how little anyone treasured what he gave and gave and gave away. With the same destructive steadiness that Kuney devoted to throwing himself about, those who took what he offered discarded too much of what they received. It seemed, truly, that he wanted them to do so. Since there was always so little to possess, it was all too inadequate for love. The mind can balk, as the heart must do, at such paltry offerings.

I came to his 'sniffle-party', as he called it, at his summons; in the morning he had called to tell me everything he insisted I come to hear again that afternoon. Two days, perhaps three, had passed since the assault of the storm had twisted and maimed the city, and by then some of the snow had been cleared away. Cars, buses, people, all had begun to slide back into place. Yet the very air was still charged with metropolitan surprise at the unexpected storm. Everyone seemed to be reeling, still, with strange pride, for they had discovered the unsuspected stamina which always accompanies havoc in a gigantic city.

Dense snow, terrible heat, prolonged rain, subway accidents, telephone strikes – these public calamities rain down on New York with the force of an epidemic's blows, seeming to render it helplessly, poignantly collective. One feels it most deeply and guiltily in time of war, yet there is exaltation in this. For such vast disorder suddenly deprives strangers of their accustomed indifference, of the habit of potential enmity, and expels one's privacy into a tougher and sweeter world of heady communion through the common affliction. The unknown neighbour who suffers from a pain he knows is not his alone, can take no refuge in the unseen drama of his solitude. When discomfort is widely shared, each of us is robbed of his anonymous agony, and we all feast together on the holiday familiarity that suddenly joins us to the surrounding strangers.

This intimacy blasts apart the common denominator, and when it is broken, the units become for a moment unequal, dislocated, distracted, perhaps lost – but they find, too, a heightened exhilaration. Curiosity and discomfort stalk the beast of loneliness, and there is a fevered delight in the chase that is felt by everyone, a giddy intoxication with everything involved in the general calamity. Each day I explored the newspapers with unusual greed and thoroughness, avid for new accounts of stalled cars, mangled telephone wires, freak footnotes to the duller statistics – an organist had found himself snowbound in an uptown cathedral, recording Bach in white, unrattled silence which no piety, no mechanical soundproofing could have rendered so perfect. All the hospitals were crowded with the many who had cracked arms and legs in slippery stumbles. I had to know every last detail of the monstrously gratifying scandal, and Kuney, who fed on scandal and gorged disaster with the glee of a mad reformer, asked for no richer season.

Huge banks of the catastrophic snow had been shored along the sides of every street, and already their whiteness was streaked and dulled by the soot that had returned to its dominance of the urban air. Orange and banana skins, the absurd harvest of garbage that always pushes through snow-banks in New York, gave strange, dilapidated spots of colour to the congested streets. It was Saturday; I did not have to work, and I could have avoided the perilous and nasty excursion through Manhattan which I chose to make. But I relished the holiday giddiness that had come loose with the discomforts of the blizzard, and early in the winter afternoon I struggled into the elephant dress of a bitter winter, boots and heavy coat and scarf, all tied and buttoned and zipped. I clumped down the stairs of my house at the lower end of Manhattan to make my awkward way through the seventy blocks that divided me from Kuney's brownstone apartment uptown. I had to take a roundabout way – some of the buses were still not running – and it seemed to take forever. At each screeching stop of the subway between stations, each halting, moaning chug of the bus, I damned myself and Kuney, too, with the unreasonable fury of the guilty, but I did not turn back.

I arrived in a scattered state, flung half-in, half-outside myself by the tug-of-war trip through the maimed city. My clothes felt heavy, my hands were numb, my hair disordered, my nose running, and this strong disarray only made me the more angry and puzzled, as I puffed up the four steep flights to Kuney's apartment, at his mastery of my time at such moments. As I came up the stairs, I could hear the bellow of his laugh, loud and high above any of the syncopated disharmony made by the afternoon visitors. With

Kuney there were none of the usual hesitations and pauses, the conversation at the start that stutters and stops. One swam, as I did then, straight into his laughter, was sucked without ceremony into the river of words that ran ceaselessly from him. And there, that afternoon, as I had felt so many times in a hundred for him and scorned and adored him, I laughed at him and despised him but, however ruinously and covetously, I did kiss him.

He held on to my shoulder: 'Come here, come right over here. Wicked girl! She's really an angel,' he went on, lowering his voice to a conspirator's hum, speaking as though I were not really there, 'but sometimes I could spank her.' For me, his voice became thick with the pasted gloom of a Puritan lament, his forehead crimped into a minstrel-show scowl of avuncular rage, and Kuney clasped his fingers together on his vast front, glared at me with heavy, impish buffoonery, ordered me to put my coat in the other room, allowed me the special favour ('Because I must have words with you later!') of sitting on his bed, of pouring him cups of tea. At once he ordered me to notice a new face he added to the thumb-tacked gallery on his walls, the glossy images of the famous, the infamous, the mediocre, the hangers-on, everyone from the avant-garde novelists to faded vaudeville stars, all of whom he knew very, very well and could call at a moment's notice to prove his intimacy if it were ever questioned. How he wore himself out in his desperate serenades under so many balconies of fame!

But before I could begin to speak with him, he had turned to a newer arrival, leaving me dizzy and enriched in that company by his unexplored intimations. His questions were part of the game. I was deprived of no real secrets, for it was the zest he gave to throwing about his balloons of secrecy that really mattered. I knew that he cared more for the having than the using, that his possession of special secrets was the great coup. But there was no Iago in him. He grew fat on the mere smell of intrigue, and the truth is that I relished feeding him the stuff of such titillation. Secrecy, the deliberate furtiveness that some admire, the complex sarabande of withdrawal and disguise – these have never attracted me for their seeming comfort. I find no safety in the slam of a door, in the closed mouth, in the private and insulated rooms of the heart. To go unnoticed – that is the great fear – and the risk of exposure is far less, to me, than the deaths of obscurity. In the glitter of Kuney's attention I could be adorned with the glamorous intimations of mystery, which his poking questions and grandiose disapproval seemed about to bring to light. How I relished his chattering invasions! I felt suddenly warmed and important, like the bored office worker who, in her uneasy concentration, takes a secret, guilty delight in the telephone's clang, the gossip's visit, the noise in the street. The accidental boon of interruption saves her from the worst enemy, herself.

And Kuney knew this, as he played out his part against mine, he knew it with all the discrediting insight which he constantly short-changed. The truth, which he somehow salvaged from the noise he made, was my need for him, though it was expressed in my sham disapproval of the tongue he seemed to deploy against my will. I see now what it was he saw. For in his teeming and cluttered world, some centre was always there, the guide with which he picked his giddy way and responded always to the cues of a subtle necessity. Perhaps it was his kindness that saw to it. He could be maliciously indiscreet, but never malignant, and I remember the many times when I found myself telling him what I had, till the moment it spilled over in my talk, claimed I would want him, loose-tongued, silly babbler, lapping up all the gossip there was and much that only wanted to be, least to know. I am afflicted the sense of betrayal as I say this, but surely he betrayed himself worst of all, more than I, who undid him in so many judgements, in the conversations I had about him, in all the varieties of scorn and indifference I heaped on the life he led.

Yet when I speak of my treachery, of his own and the world's distortions, I speak too of the joy I found in confessing to him, for I knew I took no risks, that he would demand no ransom. And I think of the scorn one feels for a confessor, in choosing him. We make him less to himself and to us by sharing the worst of what we are in the mucky barter. From it the confider withdraws, free of the ugly story; the confidant alone is left with the burden of this knowledge. And I betrayed Kuney most deeply, perhaps, by my very pretense that he forced my confessions.

Words in any and every form were his food and wine and tobacco and narcotics and his sex as well. Surely he was one of the most sexless people I have ever known not only because his grossness would seem to negate it for him, but one never thought of Kuney as needing sex, or having place for its necessary patience in his noisy life. His talk and time were always packed and cluttered with new books, unfinished manuscripts he alone had been allowed to see, unpublished novels and half-finished paintings and the first movements of new concertos. He would point portentously to his fat briefcase and say: 'You would never guess what I have in there! Blanche Knopf herself lent me her private lavender-scented galleys, and I tell you, it's nothing short of amazing.' And no amount of disinterest could keep him from telling, quickly, as though forced into revelation, exactly whose book he had. Somehow he seemed always to have read a book before the author had quite developed its plot, and he decorated each of these private spheres of work with an ornate garland of anecdote and inside information which he collected and piled hazardously high on to anything that caught his shifting attention. He read with the frenetic zeal of a bibliomane, strewing the bones and crumbs of other men's brains wherever he went. With voracious and indiscriminate greed, he made everything in print become part of his kingdom: innumerable magazines, pamphlets, papers, books, other people's letters as well as those he had received. He behaved as though the words would not exist if he did not give them the charity and labour of his attention.

In one sense, of course, this greed for all the words, that were and might be, was of some reasonable necessity to him. His infrequent and uncertain cheques for the hack writing he did, depended on exactly such mock-scholarly erudition. But his was a brazen ferocity that went far beyond exact motives. He could intoxicate himself completely, with an alcoholic's doggedness, on words alone. Curiously, in the world of frenetic drinking that Kuney moved through, his dancing attendance on all the parties and dinners and 'teas' that poured and lurched themselves daily to blurred and remorseful ends, he rarely took a drink, and had given up smoking long before I met him. There were better things to occupy him. He made his hazardous livelihood by turning out potpourri articles about everything from poetry to vanishing creams for dozens of magazines, but one never thought of him as a writer; one could hardly think of him being anything but Kuney. He was, however distraught and garbled and dizzying, the life he led and however lacking in vocation and center it seemed, he managed to turn on this unique axis with a whirling control and indefinable power of importance for everyone who knew him. Dedicated to his amusements, to his sacred irregularity, to the city he celebrated and adored, Kuney's life seemed in some ways a delicious contradiction to all the chains of routine, work, income, boredom, schedule which bound the rest of us, and perhaps some of his fascination came from the freedom he alone seemed to have won. Discipline, to him, was a threat, the dirtiest word of all.

Above all, there was a solace of possession. His apartment was not large, but every shelf, table-top, corner and closet was stuffed with his vast, mad property. Dominating it all were the books, new and old, good and bad, some read and others never opened.

The very air was thick with novels, poetry, dictionaries, memoirs, histories of art, studies of the dance, great writing sidling against garbage. He gloried in the miles of print competing for space in all his congestion. Had he read it all? He did not claim it, any more than he claimed originality for the ideas that sprouted in his talk from the roots of other minds. Yet all of it was there as the stamp and seal of his fantastic triumph, in the having and holding alone, the feat of giving the look of permanence to such clutter.

There was much more than the books all was incontestably there, it was his testimony to all the people he knew, the places he had visited, the things he had seen and done and remembered. How well I remember the towers of old theatre-programmes, the weird and worthless glass statues, Coney Island souvenirs, and there was no moving through the four narrow, bulging rooms of his flat without bumping into all manner of odd trinkets he might once have been given as whimsical Christmas jokes, into the mounds of seashells that mixed the ugly and beautiful and broken as freely as the sea that spewed them up. For him, a bare patch of space was painful, it effaced his groaning tables, and shelves. Yet for Kuney, whom I dare not call imposter, the variety of his plenty was the token of its worth, and it took on, however discordant the elements, a strange force of beauty.

Truly his pedantry had its own wild sanity. No one ever thought of him as eccentric, for what he looped and linked and piled onto himself and his home became, for all who saw it, part of his curious, giddy and contagious curiosity. In his larder of discards, everything had its necessity, forming the world he had created in order to exist in it; the fantastic crockery and lamps and chairs, the stage-gold candelabra, Victorian gargoyles, mirrors that refracted a side-show grimace, the oversized cologne bottles, ornate Edwardian statuery, ten-year-old movie magazines full of out-dated romances and pouting, marcelled starlets. Amid all this abundance he sat like the owner of a warehouse who has fallen so insanely and irrevocably in love with each subject fished up on the hook of his promiscuity, he must sit starving in the midst of his suicidal harvest, for lack of the will to sell.

It was all such a weird pantomime of solidity, and the force of it moved about with him wherever he went. Always he would arrive anywhere, usually late and hilariously apologetic, panting and clanking with the new, the shocking, the till-now unknown, crying his peddler's wares of gossip that he had stuffed into his pockets at the last party, scattering eccentric abundance with the abandon of a wild maharajah overproud of his vast pleasure dome, from which any bauble, jewel or gadget could be pulled for glittering display at a moment's notice. If Kuney's true richness could be counted only as time to be wasted, intelligence and information and words to be thrown about carelessly, frenzied plans for new editions of this or that, anthologies and literary revivals, blown ludicrously beyond their capacity to convince or dismay or enlighten, it had to be remembered that he had no other gold to give or to sell.

What he made of all this grotesque plenty was a genuine entertainment. All the absurd variety vibrated with the fun he derived from himself. And he admitted his avarice with such a confounding joy and mockery, that any solemn scorn died quickly in the face of his laughter. When I remember the way he lived, how freely he sported a sybarite's manner and covetousness, I am haunted, too, by the actual meagreness of his resources. Living always from wit to mouth, he made his talk and habits trail a fraudulent glitter behind. Constantly in debt, overdrawn at his bank, haggling for a few dollars more from this magazine or that publisher, his air of opulence was a joke that lacked the charity of truth. Despite all his casual familiarity with the best restaurants in New York, his easy delight in 'seeing everything worth seeing' from the best seats and boxes, his minute knowledge of the homes of the very rich, and the haunts where they scraped up their pleasures, this seeming baron was often penniless. He could make no actual claim to any of the grandeur New York offers in such fatty abundance. Yet he knew it all well enough, and his familiarity gave him the poise of the denizen.

Where had this connoisseur's grace been acquired? Not in his childhood, certainly. He grew up in one of a dreary, genteel row of 'two family' houses, in one of the lifeless subway streets of Queens, one of five children haggling for room in an ordinary middle-class world as far removed from the highest high-life as a Russian serf from the Czar. Yet Kuney could go, as he did so often, from cocktail parties in the lush penthouse of a gilded patroness, to dinner with his family, and never show any disturbance at making such a bizarre plunge. Kuney had no claim, born to or begotten by luck or work or tricks of temperament, to that easy indifference about money which can sometimes make, among the few of the very rich whose guilt does not equal their plenty, for a seeming ignorance of its necessity. Kuney was his own panhandler, but he spoke of money rarely, and when he did, it seemed incidental to his vaster interests. For he had, after all, entered all the inner worlds of luxury through the nod of a friend's head, through endless 'connections' and 'contacts', through the specious generosity of an expense account. Though he tippled favours, passes, gifts, left-overs continuously, he never betrayed any of the impudent wariness of the intruder as he moved through the pampered rooms, and showed none of the obsequious gratitude which his patrons might have liked to demand.

Even on this difficult winter day, when moving from home meant a strenuous energy, he had managed to lure to his side a typical tribe. I bumped and jostled in the small rooms against a celebrated pianist, a moderately successful and immoderately acidic young novelist, an elaborately sad lady who had once been a well-known soprano and was now remembered only by pedantic collectors of rasping old phonograph records. In one corner I noticed a furtive professor from Columbia whose genteel diffidence always seemed embarrassingly out of place in such worldly company, and he was speaking to a nail-chewing painter who had not been near a canvas for years but drank his way through the dear dead days of Paris with increasingly unsteady melancholy. There were also the anonymous ones whose names and faces had, like my own, never come out of a private darkness into the public light. And I, who so often despised myself for coveting this spurious intimacy with fame which Kuney seemed to provide, was there too, though I could remember all the times before when I had felt childish in coveting this disenchanting peek at the bearers of fame. But I wanted it and somehow, though Kuney trumpeted his mountebank vanities at such a brazen pitch, he succeeded in drawing us all to his side.

'Mme Grushaninov,' Kuney was saying in the hectic blast of introductions that rarely left any of the names clear, 'Mme Grushaninov, I've been dying to have you meet this girl.' He clutched my hand with the secret ferocity of an ambitious mother. 'Anna, this is a great, great moment for you. This is Ilyenka Grushaninov, someone you're very lucky to meet. What an artist! See how nice I am to you?' I nodded and smiled with perfunctory grace, as I knew he expected me to do. But I was dismayed at the need to force so simple a gesture. Who was she? I could not remember having heard the name before.

Kuney, making me accomplice, spinning his web of distracting flattery, went on: 'You're both such Dostoevskian women; you should have loads to talk about. Oh… all sorts of dark female Russian secrets. Just two little Anna Kareninas!' So that was to be my role for the afternoon; but this time I was reluctant to play. I shook her hand, and a moment later she was clutching again at the heap of beads, lace and velvet that ruffed her throat, obsessed by her banal melancholy, baring her unpleasantly regular teeth in a smile that stuttered like a silent movie. Her waxen, pampered hands – she had been, it was clear, inordinately proud of them once – fidgeted without cease. How many women like this one Kuney knew! They were part of the debris he treasured, left-overs from a day of taste that no longer enclosed them, cast now among the lampshades and the seashells and the red glass jars that only Kuney could find valuable. Perhaps, once, she had been magnificent, the artist he called her, but to me she was now only lugubrious, sunk under the betraying years, dismayed that the light of the world had turned away from her. Among Kuney's relics, this woman was like a gilt chair that had once decorated a gaudy, crowded ballroom, but now, chipped and ancient, could support no weight at all. Her eyes were embalmed in a face which had once devoured attention with an unthinking vanity, yet Kuney could speak with loud and repetitive devotion of her dead splendour, enumerate the great moments and anecdotes of her career, concerts she had given before he was born- and make it seem that somehow he had witnessed and shared all her triumphs. And it was for such a makeshift, haphazard nostalgia that this woman came to him so often, out of the cave of her memories, to live out a few of her hollow hours in the tattered patchwork shroud of the past he threw upon her shoulders.

I was repelled by her hostile eyes, which coveted my youth and despised me for it, and Kuney, seeing this, grabbed at the book I had been carrying, and saved me for the moment from Mme Grushaninov by swinging into one of his wild verbal journeys: 'How did you come to be reading this...of all things? Haven't you heard an extraordinary number of people mention his name recently, just everywhere? You know...' and his face turned sage and reflective for a moment, 'you know, I really ought to do a piece for *Woman's World* about him. After all it would be so perfect, don't you think? Nothing elaborate. But the way they'd dress it up, it would be just heaven. Divine photographs, nothing cheap. You know…the houses he lived in (Cecil could do them wonderfully, just wonderfully) and the women who sat for his portraits. I could do it in diary form. They always love that, it's so fantastically intimate.'

This, then, would become the week's focus, the new excuse ('I'm doing such an incredibly difficult thing for *Woman's World*, and they're clamouring for it, it just means work and work and work!') for leaving one party to go on to the next, full of the moment's high seriousness. Often when Kuney had talked to me of such projects, I might easily have told him, no, I didn't think there was going to be a revival of Meredith or Thackery or Turgenev, or whatever he had fastened on through some quixotic chance. I might have told him, for it was surely what I felt true, that the idea was trivial and the form he chose to give it merely a way of underwriting its triviality. But this I never dared do – or rather, I never bothered. Meanwhile, though to speak of my scepticism might have sanctioned another kind of talk, I agreed with him too easily and smiled my way out of judgement. Here, now, he was leafing through my book, scrawling illegible notes on the back of an envelope with the impatience of someone who has discovered a gigantic idea for saving mankind from war and pestilence forever, and cannot hurl himself rapidly enough into his obsessive concentration. For Kuney, this would last for but a few minutes now, but he would return to it in a hundred noisy places, lamenting the little time he could find for such work in his teeming life.

Stuffed with information bristling with allusive rejoinders, he seemed at times to have appropriated the world of art and ideas for his private abattoir and seemed to give it all the stamp of his flippant, frenzied energy. All his judgements sported a tipsy garland of extravagant superlatives which cancelled themselves out too often. A master of the small and gaudy vocabulary babbled through all the shining corridors of New York, he knew the doggerel well, the words cooked into an indigestible sauce, intoned through all the theatres, bars, museums, apartments and offices which make up that knowing world. What Kuney liked was never less than wonderful, divine, fantastic, incredible, marvellous, or enchanting and often it was all these things and more. His was one of the master hands at flinging out such rubber checks for sincerity, but he never quite bartered away all judgement for the slighter stuff of mannerism. Though Kuney had cried "divine" much more than once too often, someone was always caught up in his churning whirlpool of enthusiasm. For it all had more than a moment's useful excess, as he lived it.

Of course – of course: there was reason to the scorn with which so many spoke of him, and when the words would be said, to someone who would be sure to repeat it to Kuney, he seemed to take the greatest delight in their malice, agree too readily to the point well-made. He relished 'that absolutely wonderful, wicked tongue', and I would see him face such second-hand contempt by roaring with glee, slapping his thighs and flapping his hands and forcing everyone to laugh with him. Indignation would be impossible, hurt feelings too quiet, and Kuney was always ready to be sacrificed to the small moment rather than expose himself to pity – or change.

I think, now, as I look straight into his sun without the distorting camouflage of his shadow-play, that I consented to his destruction too easily, and the guilt sits like an unbudgeable stone in my breast. For something, I know, always escaped the jester's maw, something marred the perfect image of the dancing clown. When he laughed at me I was never hurt by him, for the specious malignance of his taunts was always part of the joke. No, the ridicule he so willingly took on was not, after all, what he deserved, and though at times I would pledge myself to small moralities, to the effort of protest and defence, I forgot them always in a lazy indifference.

By seven o'clock that winter evening, even Kuney's well of talk seemed about to go dry. No one, least of all our invalid host (if he chose to conduct his concert from bed, that was but another divertissement) had been much aware of his illness. His parties always came to a vicarious end, when there were suddenly no more cigarettes and no more wine, and someone remembered the prodding of a duller life, of pedestrian needs which had to outlaw Kuney's fun. Farewells were always prolonged, for he loathed to see people depart, and made many desperate campaigns to keep them, with his many small devices. The party's giddy pitch would rise up again in the intense and delicious hypocrisies of leave-taking. This afternoon the coda was less elaborate than usual, and most of his guests left almost at once. Perhaps because of the difficult journey we all faced now, returning to our separate lives, or because Kuney's illness had made him less ebullient than usual; perhaps out of the cold urgency that in winter shuts down too abruptly with the early doors of darkness, none of us tried to stay on. I was alone, suddenly, with Mme Grushaninov and Kuney, not quite sure why I hadn't gone along with the others, unable now to leave without an awkward break.

To keep me, as I thought, Kuney turned once again into the stern father, his special game with me, and he said with a knowing scowl: 'My dear, you've been remarkably quiet this afternoon. What's got into you, what's holding your tongue, you babbler? What's going on in your young life? Eh? Tell me – as though I don't know all about it anyway! But such silence from you, Anna! I've never heard the likes of it.' I assumed a suffering face, pretended great sadness at some unspeakable tragedy, and kneeled for a moment on his bed in a vaudeville supplication. Mme Grushaninov, amused out of her self-impassioned boredom, looked up at our pantomime, the melancholy attention hardly alive in her ashy despair at seeing the afternoon vanish, and with it, all the gossamer life that Kuney gave to her snuffed-out fame. I knew that from here she would make her way back to a dingy room in a boarding-house somewhere in the West Seventies, disappear into the heavy corridors of a grim red-rust brownstone, bereft of the transient glory she had found in Kuney's arch celebrations, return to a slow counting of her survival in the maudlin hours and days. There she would have only herself and the treasured scrapbooks on which she breathed the puzzled sighs of the forgotten celebrity, arrogant over relics which aroused no memories in others.

I felt a moment's pity now for the route she had to travel, for the cheap small tea-room she would find that reeked with a damp fog of failure and creamed cabbage and rancid gentility. But it served – it could welcome her into its anonymity. With a great straining and gathering of her faded furs, she brushed imaginary crumbs from her skirt and opened her antique beaded purse with a vast slow sighing concentration, took out a tiny initialled box from which she carried more chalk-white powder to her over-coated face. She too was kissed in turn, threatened and chided and advised by our bearded, fatherly host, and stayed for a moment longer to gulp down the last of Kuney's lavish adoration. I looked too slowly for my coat and boots, holding back my departure in the distaste I anticipated at being alone with her if we left together, at finding excuses for not remaining with her, for not sitting in a puddle of pity while she hacked out the full ransom of my youth.

But there was more to detain me that afternoon, for Kuney clutched my hand with a strange insistence. I was bewildered by the gesture, and tired by my sudden change of heart as I stared, listless and distracted and limp after the pointless frivolity that had grown like weeds in the afternoon, at the cigarette butts and the cheap wineglasses. I listened to the last of Mme Grushaninov's rustle and clump in her heavy trappings as though I too were about to descend into a dark, sad well, down the steep flights to the cold streets below. Kuney, suddenly wholly quiet, showed for the first time that he was ill. The face ambushed in his comic beard was mottled, half-flushed, half-green in a drained and sickly pallor. He blew into a handkerchief with a loud wet roar and gasped for breath. The muscles of his face, which had been bunched and taut for the party, had suddenly given way, loose in the relief of fatigue. His court was gone and the jester could now relax.

I asked him if there was anything he wanted of me before I left. But there was something else in his face which made me want to flee him, now, just as I had escaped the dreaded intimacy with Mme Grushaninov. The moment cried out for pity, but that was not, after all, what I came to him to give or to find. My pathos was touched elsewhere often enough.

Pity, against his comic screen, in full view of Kuney's need? It would be a cheat, upset the lovely applecart and turn loose the worms that crawled underneath. It might even be forced into the seriousness of love, here, of all places, where I came to escape from tenderness, from all that made me vulnerable. Pity would commit me, trap me into a dangerous quicksand of feeling, throw down the circus tents of Kuney's merry no-man's-land and leave me with no place to hide. And I, who could not, I thought, afford such expense of spirit, would not help him ruin the game.

To hold his hand, remain with him, to expose my unacknowledged need for him in giving way to his need for me, I should have to reject the delicious inconsequence of the afternoon, and abandon hope of finding escape in his banter ever again. How could I give up the solacing, easy gossip he fed me, tear down the fluttering ribbons of bright talk and see the dull walls as they were, consign to the attic's dust all the baubles and rings and toys and clattering bells of his free and giddy carnival? I came to Kuney for respite from solemnities, to have the music of his superficiality drown out, for a time, my endless quarrel with myself. I came to him for the evasion I could find in the party that was always there, and not to grant him the supreme gift of feeling. How could I give all, all of that easy gaity away for the sour and steady commitment of pity?

The silence of the room, heavy and depressing now with the sudden end of voices, dragged me down with the demanding weight of its quiet, with the threatening tick-tick-tick of my ordinary life. All the forced sad rhythms of penance that are heard so steadily in New York were sounding more loudly with each moment. Here, in this room that lived for noise, I now found only crouching silence, quiet as a dead heart, and I knew that if I stayed, all the unkempt and awkward underground of myself would begin to erupt with the pity, even the love, I might discover in myself for Kuney. Yet he knew how reluctant I was to turn and meet the shocking openness I saw in him at that moment, and because he knew this, knew that I had deliberately chosen not to give him what he wanted, now, he could not plead. For one moment longer he looked at me, his face loose and loveless in its flaccid immobility, and he seemed in this moment, which he quickly drowned out with a giggling sneeze, to want to beg me for the rare mercy of concern. And I refused him everything but my guilt, which I would keep to myself. Only a void was there now, and he filled it quickly with the agitated joviality of his familiar self.

'All right, all right, I know you're sneaking off to some sordid assignation, you Village assignator you, and you don't want me to guess where you're going. Heavens what a life you lead!' he howled and hooted his mocking farewell as I strapped on my boots and put on my coat. I comforted myself by remembering that he would begin dialing a number even before I had gone through the door, berating, prying, stretching the last morsels of the afternoon with his gossip, that within an hour ten of the friends who had not come to him that afternoon would have ten differing accounts of the party, of the painter's drinking and Mme Grushaninov's dull poignance and the professor's timidities, of my silence. ('Very odd, I just know something wild is going on in that girl's life. Who do you suppose she's getting involved with now? It couldn't be that awful boy again. I've told her and told her it will do her no good.')

And thus I left, vainglorious through my easy eminence in his talk, knowing that this was my reward for coming, in the number of times my name would soon be crossing all the miraculous wires. As I hit the cold air of the winter's night, depressed as always by the too-early fall of the sun, I felt stung back into myself and deflated, as I always did when I left Kuney and became again an ordinary person making her way through icy and dirty streets to the subway, carrying a book under a frayed sleeve, going back to huddle, in a badly-heated apartment, over a supper of eggs and toast and cocoa. I could not let myself think that I took away with me something which I might, perhaps, have needed to give, and I struggled to blow my nose, tie my scarf, pull off my glove, wrestle with my purse, find the right coin and be rushed through the underground tunnels, back into the skin of my sameness. Perhaps I had not, after all, been remiss.

Kuney's illness had not been serious. His cold was soon over, and he moved back into all the familiar lines of commotion that kept him occupied. His vitality and his humour, as always, saved him from the worst perils of his melodrama, and his by now famous walk through the blizzard soon took its place in the clutter of his talk, adding to the tangled spaghetti-strands of remarks, comments, quips and puns, which he could neither discard nor treasure but which was, like the rest, part of his variety. All through the remaining months of winter, through the dead-end bleakness of February that finds everyone weary and older and tired and living on the iron rim of the uncertain weather, I saw him often, and knew I could find him in all the places where my own restlessness, and fear of empty time, would drive me – and that he was often to be found in many other parts of the city which I could not reach or know. I could not count so many as my friends; I could scarcely have wished it. But Kuney's tireless lust for acquisition, of people and books and talk and words, grew more ravenous through its constant satisfaction, like a stomach that enlarges in a more gluttonous hunger with every banquet.

For me those months were a disheartening, restless succession of shoddy disenchantments, but Kuney never disappointed me by becoming unpredictable. His consistency, his mockery, his astoundingly even temper took on greater and greater importance for me as the rest of my world seemed always to be ebbing and breaking and wavering. His presence remained the bright steadiness among all the shoddy phantoms of expectation and change which shadowed the rest of my life. The others were never like him: they were bored with me, or they bored me, they demanded attention for the dirty, anxious privacy of themselves too often, they made scenes, were difficult, left me and came back to me always at the wrong moments, demanded my love and my time and my sympathy and even my uncertainty too selfishly – or denied me their bounty when I most coveted it. The rest of my world? How few there were who didn't compete with me and insult me, pry and poke at me, blow hot and cold in the intricate breathing that makes one life exist within another.

But Kuney, the tireless entertainer, the clown who could always repeat his performance on demand, if he could but find another audience he gave me no such troubles. No matter how many times I would grow impatient and even angry with him because I had to dial his number so often before reaching him, I knew that he was there to bed had, to be disturbed, bothered and badgered to be always himself at the other end of the telephone. He was always worth the effort of persistence. For how could his time not be ripe for invasion? In his erratic periods of work, his habits were as disordered and contrivedly disarranged as his possessions and his enthusiasms. Kuney had to take the risk, always, of not knowing what he had in hand: it was much safer than finding out how little capital he possessed, and how much he was depleting it. With ghoulish delight, he gloried in the steady mortality decreed by the bored and fickle arbiters of New York journalism.

He always could announce pontifically which magazine had 'done' Mondrain first, which had fired the original explosive in the overmined Melville mountain. He knew without a doubt the precise moment when the James 'revival' went into decline, that Stendhal was old hat, Cocteau a bore, and Gênet the newest, freshest genius of them all. And he knew, too, that Theda Barra was 'still, amazingly, wonderfully goodlooking at her age,' and that secret, if such it was, had not escaped him. Never less than fully informed, he was always more than certain when what would happen, and where next. Since his crystal ball seemed to contain so much more than any clairvoyant could wish to see, his writing was always corrupted by the frivolous extravagance of his prophecies and pronouncements. In his erratic, anxious desire to be heard, he always gave the game away.

Early in April Kuney's talk was in characteristic disarray – with articles he was writing, ideas for elaborate globs of magazine culture he hoped to sell in five or six skyscrapers, odd hack jobs he had to fulfull within the next twenty-four hours. He was writing an article about Brooklyn antique shops, and another about primitive painters in Haiti and he was peddling plans for three elaborate Christmas anthologies which he said would make his and the publisher's fortune. Mostly, he was writing reviews of third-rate novels for a Sunday book supplement. His talk spilled over with the souvenir gossip he carted away from three-hour lunches at the Colony and the Plaza and the Pavillion, when the bills were discreetly signed away by the stylish editors of rival magazine who always said of him, 'We love Kuney, we couldn't adore him more, he's such heaven, such a sweetie, such a divinely amusing lamb.' They courted him and fed him, paid for him like a pampered bear, as they nibbled at his savory malice about each other. That spring he was in touch with me often, for he claimed never to have gone underground to Brooklyn, where I had been born, and I became his makeshift library for the article about antique shops.

Most mornings, just as I had settled down to my desk, the telephone would interrupt whatever I might be doing, and there would be Kuney's voice, bellowing 'Brooklyn! My dear, it's the one thing I can't, simply can't understand about you. I wouldn't dream of setting foot in the dreary place, and you're remarkably human to have come from there. Just too awful to think about, but I must, this silly piece they're forcing me to do, and you must tell me exactly what you know about all those horrible divine shops.' But the minutes would talk themselves into half-hours before I could tell him anything. How I loved his bombast, his flattery! I would tempt him to pile absurdity on absurdity, which happily kept me from my duller work and gave me sweet knowledge of fresh secrets and disasters, which he had learnt the night before. In the sacred dishevelment he practiced, he would delay writing until the last minute, interrupting himself constantly to call on friends, to plead and moan, knowing that we would all hear him out and giggle away his spurious agony about the impossible task.

Always, he would settle down to the drudgery of his ordeal at two o'clock in the morning, after the holy round of parties and tête-à-tête was done, the last confidences tucked away, when even he had stayed a bit too long at the last of the last parties. Only at such an hour, when all the avenues of evasion were finally shut, when the telephone could not be used freely, could he face the grim struggle with his type-writer. His manuscripts were a mosaic, formed out of the very disorder by which he lived, words, and sentences and ideas scrambled together from notes written on a dozen scraps of paper stuffed in odd pockets and books, from magazines and dictionaries he pulled out to distract and amuse himself, to lessen the stubborn blank of the writing paper. After he had tortured himself thus, through the lonely night, he would hurl the mass of paper from him and, with morning, his fingers itched greedily to the telephone, freed now by the start of the normal day, and he could join his friends in lament for his sweat and his sleeplessness.

'What I've been through! You'd never, never guess.' And I would pretend then to urge him for the story – for this was the true reward of his labours. Whatever tears and terrors might have happened in the merciless solitude of the night, were scattered by the morning's familiar fun. It became, in his hyperbole, a vigil, a walk through hell, a monumental labour, and finally still another joke on himself, which he was the first to point up and laugh at. His travesty of work had such a wild implausibility, it became a soothing antidote to my own over-solemnised failures, and gave me that heightened moment of superiority – surely anything was serious compared to his mockery? – when I most needed it. I knew that by the end of his wanderings that day, his ordeal forgotten in playing out so many new charades, he would go home and demand nothing more. Yet such vigils were part of what I made him, for myself. I could never think of Kuney asleep like others. How could he, so dependent upon a constant agitation, succumb to the immobility of sleep, or give in to its stillness? The independent heresies of a dream were not for him.

Through the months of spring, on into the relentless heat of summer, I thought often, with a grudging care, of the many such nights he lashed himself through still another article, another book-review, another mound of notes. I began to feel that perhaps he was paying too exorbitant a price in his frivolous spending of himself. I had heard, but not from him, that his health was bad. Someone had said something to someone else about his heart, but this seemed, as the rule made it seem in everything about Kuney, no cause for more than an ordinary kind of alarm. It seemed more serious that I was being told his stock was falling at some of the magazines which had been favouring him for so long. And he must have known, though he could never admit such anxiety, that the impulsive and arbitrary tastes and favours of those editors were even more impermanent than his own short-lived dedications – that he was, indeed, a taste rather than a person to these powers who could not exist without frequent change.

Kuney's spongey availability to shifts of taste and favour, his facility at a one-hour mastery of sophisticated clichés on any subject, his terror that intellectual sobriety might stamp him dull, his brash inside knowledge about every pen and brush and piano in New York – these were the goods the editors bought from him, a mobile store among many in the vast marketplace. If his larder seemed to be growing thin and stale, they could always go elsewhere. True, the editors were adept at taking the cheap unsorted plenty of his gossipy erudition, and turning it into the listening, transient wonders buried in their pages. But theirs was, after all, a more conscious cunning than anything he could use in counterattack. They merely granted him the license of his useful prodigality.

He could never threaten them with the thing he most needed and wanted and missed – an indispensable permanence of presence. The mirrors that tinkled on his person caught and reflected a hundred images at once, but they were, after all, so much glass. It was his own doing, this specious value he had placed on the slaggy abundance of his tongue and brain, as though it were one way of keeping anyone from going beneath the multitudinous, dizzying surface. The jester who excels in his derision of reality must, finally, find his own inevitable place in it, and become the pawn of his own game. Measure for measure, the world that found use for Kuney – and I was part of it – had finally to repay him in brutal kind with the very frivolity he acclaimed and lived as principle.

Yet luckily, he escaped such final, ruinous humiliation with the most macabre jest of all – his death. Though the very nature of epithet tempts me to put aside his dazzling devaluation of himself, I know that when he was alive I could never see him in any light but the glare he turned on himself. Kuney's heart, so stuffed with the strange goods of his huge abundance, gave out on the hottest day of his fortieth year, in a swampy August when not even a cat crawled along the scorched pavements, and he alone, it seemed, had not fled his beloved city. This sweating behemoth was still the only possible arena for Kuney, for his last needs – and his defiance of needs any longer. However oblique I insist his image of himself really was, he must have known that he could not last through such days, that the taxing and staggering climb to his apartment, the senseless pursuit of people he kept up, even in such weather, would take the very life out of him.

I, with the others, had taken his energy so much for granted, I could not think he would ever come to a halt – any more than I can, even now, imagine that any of the wheels of New York will stop their grinding while I witness it. If I ever allowed myself to question their self-generating immortality, if I fluttered with fear that the subway wouldn't come, the elevator not start, the bus stall for good, the mail not be delivered, the telephone unable to ring, the garbage left uncarted, traffic lights fail, department stores not open – if I could allow myself the heresy of thinking that all the noise of those necessary mechanical birds could go dead, I am certain that madness would smother me, corruption would leer and taunt at me out of a million faces. In New York, all the beasts of implausibility wait to devour you, and only the most carefully preserved credulity can keep them at bay.

And when, in crisis, that seemed to be giving out, as it did that summer, I could suspend madness by leaving, or knowing that I could leave. I could pack my life into suitcases and carry it to a world of less oppressive rhythms. But Kuney's devotion was more total, and necessarily more hazardous. Stuck and soldered to the city's wild and devouring variety, Kuney was the bird that must lose all brightness if it dare abandon the native air. All the fraudulent, conflicting colours that composed Kuney's desperate harlequin elegance depended too much upon the accidents of reflection. Yet together they were so much of a piece, the least rent or change would make a fatal wound, the slightest scratch open the gates to deadly haemorrhage, and his nakedness would be exposed mercilessly to the howling mob. His luck, finally, came in the ease of his lonely death, where exposure could no longer threaten him. And I, now that I give him my pity and perhaps a form of love, here, with the words and wonder that I scatter after him now, remember how close to the surface his ruin always lay. I wonder if he could have taken, in life, what I grant him so guiltily and in such equal abundance now. I had seen him for the last time at a party, that treacherous element in which he was always most at home, and I remember it well. I had gone there out of brash need, for I had one thought myself in love with the host, and knowing that Kuney would be there, I felt his presence would help me in my brazen nostalgia.

In the sweltering room on Madison Avenue, overcrowded, steaming in the heat with too many clever, embarrassed, fidgeting people whose shifty eyes called the thin bluff of their poised remarks, he was as always the tittering, tireless master of a purposeless celebration, and even the host was shadowed by Kuney's lusty eminence. I came in and found Kuney talking to a gaunt man whose face was vaguely known to me from similar parties, and I heard his 'Now, now, you know perfectly well she won't ever finish that novel. You know it perfectly well. I saw the first five chapters, hot off that short-circuiting typewriter of hers, and I tell you... And somehow, as always, the telling of the one story was yoked to still another man who had wandered into Kuney's large and attentive circle, to bask in his banter, feast on his seductive legend, his noisy verbal variety, now trumpeted most loudly when there were many to hear such crescendo. 'Oh, how lovely to see you, of course, of course I remember you! I heard the nicest things yesterday about your paintings, you know, from the Modern Museum people, and I wouldn't be at all surprised if...' Kuney's voice and face fell into his familiar, conspiratorial hum of warning and prophecy, that melody of trouble he delighted to sound: 'But as for that dealer you've been talking to, I'd be very careful, and don't ask me how I happen to know you've been seeing him but you can't hide that kind of...' Brighter and louder the rings of talk sped and scattered and looped through the room, whirling over and around all the lively people, scooped up in his busy hands, made to listen and to laugh.

In an hour I had gone straight into the stream of disgrace that always drowns such cocktail parties, finally, and I moved about the room slowly, with the unsteady precision and stilted coherence of the wary drunk, free for the moment, forgetting how bitter the stale remorse and regret, the dusty recapitulation would taste the next day. Time became a shambles and dragged me into its dust as my voice joined the chorus of drunken, shrill confessors. But Kuney, as he could so often do, kept straight to his sober and giddy centre, kept me standing on my feet with his reproachful attentiveness and observing of everyone in the room, and perhaps he alone preserved me from the more treacherous and dingy traps I could set for myself, as he had done so many times before. I do not deny my flagrant indifference to the point of light he held burning, burning through his peculiar artifice. But I remember how he gave me his hand, in the times I would stumble near him, and hold me steady for the moment.

I remember, if only in this oblique echo of what might have been done, that in those splintery moments of over-sharp and false clarity which drunkenness grants sometimes in the very midst of its most tawdry, deranging muddles, I saw his face seem ill and tired to me, and I began, at one moment when still another haphazard conversation had been bloated to bursting with rising gallons of intensity, to ask him why. But the question was lost somewhere, dissolved in the fifth drink too many, in a proud, idiot's retreat from the dishevelment of someone near me, greater than my own and somehow sobering for the moment, and finally there was only the need to escape quickly before all my dignity had collapsed.

'All you terrible people' I heard him howling, like a comic Savonarola, as I made my wild flight from the whirling room. 'Where is that girl going off to? Anna, Anna, where are you going, come right back here! Anna...' I heard him calling my name as I waited for the elevator, but I could not return to that room again, not with the fragile enchantments of my drunkenness clattering and falling all around me. Could he have wanted me then, as I had used him, as I had come to him so often? Perhaps he needed my disorder, then, as the precarious proof of his wholeness? Could he have wished, then, that my drunkenness might pry pity loose from me, that the hand I had taken away and held forever back on the winter day, when all frivolity had been eclipsed in that brief, unresolved moment of his need, would now, finally, go out to him, coerced by a shabby violence? But I did not know, I had not been told, and he could ask for nothing even then. My capricious morality gave me no assurance. My name was the last word I heard sound out from that familiar babbling voice.

In the street, as I signalled for a taxi with an impatient hand, the desolate weight of my undisplayed self took over, and later, scattering my clothes from door to bed as I lurched towards the ignominious forgiveness of sleep, I wondered in a resentful, prodding moment, why he had called out to me as he did. I was asleep before I could begin my caring. Kuney was dead a week later, when the heat had driven me to the country. But now my pity is not my own. I did not, after all, manage to avoid him to the last.

Acknowledgements

My first and last thanks must go to David Bell – the son of Pearl Kazin Bell and Daniel Bell. We have never met, although we did make some tentative and in the end unsuccessful plans to meet in London when David was over for an Academic History conference (David is a professor of History at Princeton University). I am sure we will meet before too long. I found David by a sudden spontaneous Google search a year or so ago when I first began to think about this book, and from my first e-mail, and throughout this project he has been supportive, kind and generous in so many ways. The straight-forward, understated life of his mother, Pearl, which he sent to me and which adds so much to this book, made me realise what a remarkable woman Pearl was and deepened my understanding of just how and why Dylan responded to her.

In my researches I have once again revisited Dylan's biographers and read again Constantine Fitzgibbon's 1965 'official' biography. Paul Ferris, a Swansea man raised and schooled in the same environment as his subject produced his invaluable, deeply researched and investigative biography in 1977 with a new revised edition in 2000. He went on to write, at her behest, a biography of Dylan's wife, Caitlin (1994) and then to edit Dylan's voluminous Letters which came out first in 1985 and in a magisterial enlarged edition in 2000. And in 2003 Andrew Lycett came up with *Dylan Thomas – A New Life* which despite all that had gone before managed to offer just that. All these books have been invaluable and I also used Caitlin's own autobiography *Caitlin: A Warring Absence*, that George Tremlett edited together from many hours of taped interviews.

In my Notes to the letters I thank two booksellers in particular but I would like to tip a wink to all my bookselling colleagues who, during the rich and rewarding forty years I plied our wonderful trade, have nudged Dylan Thomas materials my way.

Thanks too to Richard Davies and all at Parthian Books, and my friend Wyn Thomas who first suggested the title.

And lastly huge thanks to all my family, older and young who tolerate my excesses and give me joy.

Jeff Towns,
Swansea 2013